BEYOND GREATNESS

Four Thoroughbred Legends

Charles Justice

authorHOUSE®

AuthorHouse™
1663 Liberty Drive
Bloomington, IN 47403
www.authorhouse.com
Phone: 1-800-839-8640

First published by AuthorHouse 10/18/2011

ISBN: 978-1-4634-4423-5 (e)
ISBN: 978-1-4634-4424-2 (hc)
ISBN: 978-1-4634-4425-9 (sc)

Library of Congress Control Number: 2011913602

Printed in the United States of America

The Moving Finger writes; and, having writ,
Moves on: nor all your Piety nor Wit
Shall lure it back to cancel half a Line,
Nor all your Tears wash out a Word of it.

-- Omar Khayyam
Rubaiyat
Quatrain LXXI
(Fifth Edition)

Rendered in English by
Edward Fitzgerald

In loving memory of

my maternal grandmother,

Susan McCue Reid
(1886 – 1973)

my uncle,

Harry Carleton Reid
(1909 – 1978)

and to my incomparable feline friends,

Max
(1976-1988)

Sweet Pea (Peetie)
(1992 – 2007)

Henry
(1993 – 2010)

Contents

Preface

My previous book on Thoroughbreds, The Greatest Horse of All: A Controversy Examined, was dedicated to my mother, Eleanor Reid Justice.

I dedicate this book to the only two additional people who unstintingly contributed to my welfare and development: my maternal grandmother, Susan McCue Reid, and my uncle, Harry Carleton Reid.

While growing up, I always imagined that I gave them due respect and love for all they did for me. With the increased wisdom of greater age, I realize that I did not approach the respect and love for them that they deserved.

They constantly worked, alongside my mother, to help ensure that I had a more complete and satisfying life than did they.

For all that, whatever success this book may achieve will be little recompense for their efforts.

However, it is all that I can now give, and so I hereby gratefully dedicate it to their memories with a love greater than can be expressed.

Charles J. Justice
Bloomington, Indiana
April 24, 2010

Introduction

The four horses of the apocalypse may be better known in literature, but of one fact we may be certain – they were not as swift as the four principal Thoroughbreds chronicled herein!

Colin, Man o' War, Ruffian and Landaluce each ran the figurative "hole in the wind" virtually each time they raced. Each was his or her own unique point of reference for the decade in which they ran.

This book uniquely compares them, grouped by gender, age and in their chronological racing order – Colin and Man o' War as juvenile colts, followed by Ruffian and Landaluce as juvenile fillies. The comparison is generally informal. It is not intended to single out one horse of either pair as the greater. The reader must always remember the educational rather than the critical value intended in these comparisons.

If anything, the comparisons herein are guides for those wishing to do serious studies of thoroughbred performance via the rather challenging task of working with samples. Thoroughbred data samples are invariably small, being far less than thirty items, and they thus offer unique challenges in terms of unbiased interpretations. This book frequently stresses that fact.

Within the juvenile (two-year-old) age group of these four horses, only one race in a collective thirty-two was lost. That loss can, and has been, reasonably charged to jockey misjudgment rather than to equine inability.

The event was the Sanford Memorial, run as the fourth race at Saratoga Race Track in Saratoga Springs, New York on Wednesday, August 13, 1919.

The eventual winner of the six-furlong sprint, Upset, beat the then undefeated Man o' War. The winning time was 1:11:20, and Man o' War finished a half length back. It was his singular loss in a stellar two-year career of twenty-one races.

There are valid reasons for comparing these specific four champions during only their juvenile or two-year-old season and for limiting the primary comparisons to just these horses – with honorable mention given to five other thoroughbreds.

The first and basic reason is the sad fact that Landaluce, like a scintillating meteor fated to display only ephemeral brilliance, died shortly after the fifth race of her juvenile year. She enjoyed no further chance to validate her tremendous potential.

By then she had won five races in five starts with a cumulative margin of forty-six and one-half lengths, a previously unheard of accomplishment – not achieved even by the immortal Ruffian. However, hairs are now admittedly being split since Ruffian's cumulative length wins totaled forty-five and three-quarters for five races.

A second reason for these limited comparisons is to avoid any so-called era effects. I do not remotely accept the arguments that one cannot compensate for such effects. Their existence, or lack thereof, will be examined in chapter nine.

However, the notoriety gained by presumed era effects is such that it has decided me against including the great Secretariat within the primary colt comparisons.

His record will be examined, but he will not be directly measured against the two principal colts of this study, Colin and Man o' War, except cursorily. He and four other horses receive recognition via honorable mention in chapter eight.

Sysonby, whose juvenile season was 1904, certainly deserves more detailed consideration because he was a remarkable runner. For reasons beyond presumed era effects, he will not be compared on the same level with Colin and Man o' War.

The primary two colts and two fillies discussed herein were, in my opinion, arguably the greatest two-year-old thoroughbreds of the twentieth century. Admittedly, they were all North American thoroughbreds, but I feel that is scarcely a limitation. One cannot include every meritorious thoroughbred since Matchem, Eclipse or Herod in a study such as this and maintain tidiness or sanity. This is not saying that other horses from other countries were not as good. It is highly doubtful that they were better.

The fillies deserving honorable mention are First Flight, La Prevoyante and Personal Ensign, in century chronological racing order. Reasons for their not being chosen on the same level as Ruffian and Landaluce are discussed in chapter eight.

For readers unfamiliar with Landaluce, and there may be many, she was probably Ruffian's equivalent. Perhaps because she ran only as a juvenile has she been greatly ignored. Hopefully the data analysis of her five races will help substantiate this claim.

The primary reason for not including Personal Ensign in a more detailed analysis is that she ran, and won, only two races during her juvenile year of 1986. Two races provide too small a sample with which to perform meaningful data comparisons.

Since linear trend analysis (LTA) is one of two primary data analysis tools used in this career summary, Personal Ensign cannot, in principle, be justly included with the other fillies.

The reason is that two solitary data points in a linear trend analysis, no matter where they fall, always determine a straight line. A perfect straight line gives an unrealistic portrayal of real-life data. It does not allow calculating a so-called standard error of the mean, or estimate (SEE). Thus, perfect straight trend lines cannot be used.

Close examination of the past performance records of First Flight and La Prevoyante (a Canadian filly) militates against considering these excellent horses as equivalent either to Ruffian or to Landaluce. Thus, their records are compared on an honorable mention level.

Additionally, including First Flight could cause the "era effect" accusation to rear its ugly, if not mythological, head since she raced as a juvenile in 1946. Enough such accusations abound without inviting them. Their oft' misguided, stentorian cause need not be furthered herein.

Last, this study concentrates solely on the juvenile season because it is generally neglected in favor of the sophomore or three-year-old season. Much of the reason for this neglect centers on the American Triple Crown races: the Kentucky Derby, the Preakness and the Belmont.

These events generally hold center stage within the realm of thorough-bred racing, and they are open only to three-year-olds.

However, the juvenile year is certainly a valid prognosticator of great careers. Since it is generally neglected, I've chosen to build a unique study solely around it.

The following chapter gives an overview of how the main portion of the book will be developed, but a further preliminary comment regarding eras is appropriate.

The Largely Mythical Era Effect

Many would-be racing pundits harp on so-called era effects. My feeling is that these are basically bogus arguments contrived by those who simply do not wish any comparisons to be made between their favorite thoroughbred, often Man o' War, with competitors racing several decades or more later.

Seven arguments against the era effect's existence were described at length in *The Greatest Horse of All: A Controversy Examined* (1), here-after cited as GHA. They will not be repeated here.

Only three of those factors probably influenced the run times for horses racing early in the twentieth century: foal crop, steel shoes (racing plates) and ostensibly slower tracks.

However, equitable adjustments can be made for these effects, as also discussed in GHA.

After all, comparing thoroughbred runners is not the same as, for example, comparing the Fokker Dr.I tri-plane of World War I with the Navy F6F Hellcat of World War II. Such comparison would indeed be ludicrous, unless it was merely a side-by-side tabulation of how the two aircraft differed physically on factors such as engine weight and power, climb and dive speed, or yaw, pitch and roll characteristics, etc.

One certainly could not devise a proper numerical rating scale that would justly compare the Fokkers with the naval planes of WWII regarding fighting ability. There are no valid comparisons *of this type* because, in this case, an era effect *does certainly exist*.

That era effect is comprised of the entire technology, science, engineering knowledge and manufacturing skills that were available during the latter war as opposed to the former. This is a basic nature-of-the-times issue.

However, the basic genetic nature of the racehorse has not changed significantly, certainly not during the interim from the beginning to the end of one century. And since valid compensations can be made for any effects the three stated factors might have had on horses from earlier years, there is no real argument against such comparisons.

Besides, the very people who rail the loudest against comparisons automatically proceed to make them with their ensuing breath simply by statements such as: "However, Man o' War was better than Secretariat!"

That is a comparison – based upon personal opinion only. What is its objective basis? Certainly the numbers left for posterity by these great champions in terms of distances run and times taken to run them, do not confirm the obvious superiority of Man o' War over Secretariat. *Au contraire*, if you'll pardon my French.

The past performance records of both horses are available for scrutiny. Do the comparisons yourself. I have merely suggested basic methods which will make such comparisons more organized and logical and will help remove the subjective element that most people use when judging thoroughbred ability.

At the same time, as will be repeated in further discussion, by no means do I believe that the numbers found in past-performance lines speak the *entire truth* about a given equine runner's greatness.

The numbers are merely the residue left after numerous chance factors converge. Numbers only allow a glimpse of the creature's true greatness to peek through into the otherwise often drab and distorted world of human perception and recognition.

In this regard, one is prudent to recall the idea of the semanticist, Alfred Korzybski, on such matters – that *the map is not the territory*.

The foregoing caveats stated, let us begin exploring what small-sample data can specifically disclose about four truly incomparable thoroughbreds.

Prediction is difficult, particularly about the future.
-- Niels Bohr

CHAPTER 1

This chapter gives an overview of how the four principal thoroughbreds in this study will be discussed. Of necessity, basic statistics must be used around which to make objective discussions or comparisons of past performance data. There is no other way to draw remotely unbiased conclusions concerning the relative merits of one horse versus another, especially when sample sizes are small – as they are in this study.

However, the primary purpose of this effort is *not to judge one horse against another* as 'greatest of all time'. The limitations on humans making value judgments based on statistics are generally discussed and cautioned against in any basic text.

The comparison methods used herein serve primarily as a guide for readers concerned about how to make *objective judgments* regarding thoroughbred greatness. This book is more about suggestions than carved-in-granite conclusions.

You will find no statements herein that Horse A is better than Horse B. Statistics, in fact, *cannot validly make such statements*. Statistics usually derives a bad name because statements purporting to compare quality between any individuals – horses or otherwise – are erroneously attached to it. Statistics tests hypotheses only. It cannot validly comment on comparative greatness – period!

An effective way to introduce the basic statistical concepts used herein is via an example of importance in thoroughbred racing history.

The alluded to event is the 1967 Woodward Stakes, held as the seventh race at Aqueduct Race Track on Saturday, September 30 of that year.

By the consensus of many racing pundits, that particular Woodward featured three of the greatest three-year-old colts of the past century. They were Dr. Fager, Buckpasser and Damascus. That race has, in fact, often been called the race of the century.

The Blood-Horse, Inc.(2) rated these horses as sixth, fourteenth and sixteenth, respectively, among the one-hundred greatest Thoroughbreds of the 20th Century.

Many readers may not know the results of the 1967 Woodward. Even if you do, it is interesting and instructive to apply some basic statistics and attempt to "predict" the race results, even though the outcome is known. The actual race results can then be compared with the prediction. This is probably as good a way as any to see immediately how statistics can safely be applied and what its limitations are.

This approach also highlights the advantages and pitfalls of all such statistical methods regarding whether they accurately mirror reality.

Linear Trend or Regression

Before examining the race data, some basic groundwork must be established. We begin by explaining what is meant by a linear trend line. Figure 1 displays such a line specifically tailored to this example.

Figure 1

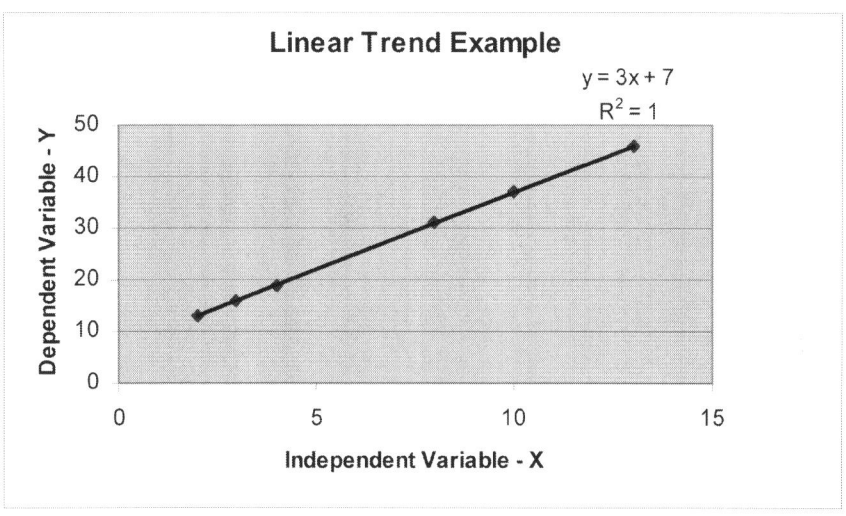

The trend line in Figure 1 was *designed* to fit its data points perfectly. Look near the upper-right-hand corner of Figure 1. You see the equation $y = 3x + 7$ and, beneath it, the R^2 value 1.00.

A value of 1.00 for R^2, called the *Coefficient of Determination* or COD, means that the straight line falls *exactly through each data point* it was intended to predict. That's logical because the equation was designed to do just that for this example.

Using Microsoft Excel, two columns of data were placed on the same spreadsheet. In a column of cells labeled 'X,' the numbers 2, 3, 4, 8, 10 and 13 were entered. In the column of cells immediately adjacent and to the right of the 'X' column, the numbers were generated by Excel according to the pre-entered formula shown in Figure 1: $y = 3x + 7$. This column was labeled 'Y'.

Thus, for $x = 2$, the y value 13, or $(3x + 7)$, was generated by Excel. Similarly, the remaining five values for Y were generated according to the values entered for x.

In this case, the resulting straight line *must* perfectly fit the data. Statisticians often use the fancier name *linear regression* when referring to such linear plots. But, as my grandmother Reid liked to say, "However you slice it, it's still bologna!" By any name, the plot is simply interpreted by noting that the '3' multiplying x indicates the *slope* of the line (how fast it rises) while the '7' is called the *y-intercept*.

Study the graph, and you'll see that if the straight line were extended backward to where it intersects the y-axis, that point would fall seven units above the x-axis. Similarly, if you begin at any given value of x and move one unit to the right along the x-axis, you will find that the line rises three units parallel to the vertical or y-axis. That is the precise meaning of the slope value, three, in this example. There is *nothing else to know* regarding the placement and orientation of straight lines in such trend analyses.

It is beneficial, however, to know that the horizontal or x-axis is traditionally used to show values of the *independent variable* while the vertical or y-axis is used for locating the corresponding *dependent variable* values. For racing data, *distances* run by a given horse are independent variables, and the corresponding y values, the dependent variables, are the *predicted times* that the given horse will take to run those distances.

Excel's LINEST routine produces ten numbers, arranged in a two-column-by-five-row table for a simple linear regression such as Figure 1 simulates. Only four of these ten values are needed for a basic interpretation of the output; these values are highlighted in Table 1 and are explained in the accompanying text.

In real life, straight line trends seldom, if ever, fit data points perfectly. This is principally because many random factors influence how a given Y value is generated from a given X value, as opposed to the example contrived for Figure 1.

Let us see how all this applies to the basic past performance data of Dr. Fager, Buckpasser and Damascus and then try to determine the results for the 1967 Woodward based on this analysis. The data used herein to produce linear trend lines or other statistical models for a given horse were obtained from the book *Champions*, published in 2000 by Daily Racing Form (3), unless otherwise noted.

Table 1 gives the LINEST output for Buckpasser based on his

complete set of racing data, *excluding the Woodward results*, for 1967, since we must exclude what we wish to predict later. Buckpasser ran five other races that year. We will use these results to predict how long it will take Buckpasser to run ten furlongs (1.25 miles), the length of the Woodward.

Table 1
LINEST Results for Buckpasser's 1967 Races

Regression Constants	LINEST Column 1	Regression Constants	LINEST Column 2
Slope	107.91	Intercept, I	-13.19
Slope Standard Error	0.7555	Standard Error of I	0.9576
R^2 (COD)	0.9998	Standard Error of the mean	0.3534
F	20396.41	df	3
Regression Sum of Squares	2547.18	Residual Sum of Squares	0.3746

From Table 1, we see that Buckpasser's linear regression equation, using only the slope and intercept values highlighted in row 1, is:

$$\hat{y} = 107.91x - 13.19$$

The y-circumflex, $\hat{y}$, is a statistics convention indicating that it is a *predicted value* (of time) based on the equation, as opposed to an *actual* run time. The values in the four highlighted cells are the *only ones needed* from the LINEST output to completely interpret simple regression equations such as this. The other values are 'niceties.'

Two values in Table 1 remain to be explained. They are the R^2 or *coefficient of determination* in column two, row three, and the *standard error of estimate (SEE)*, or *standard error of the mean*, as it is also known, in column four, row three.

The coefficient of determination indicates how well the straight line predicts the data trend. In this case, when the value of the COD is multiplied by one hundred, it is directly converted to a percent. The conversion gives 99.98 percent. It means that the linear trend line for Buckpasser's data accurately predicts 99.98 percent of his changes in running times based on changes in distance run. This is an extraordinarily high prediction accuracy compared to most real-world data. It will be seen to hold reasonably true for all racing data described herein.

The standard error of estimate value, 0.3534, is basically the standard deviation to be expected in the given data prediction. Using this example, if you substitute the value 1.25 for 'x' in the given equation, it predicts that Buckpasser's expected time for a ten-furlong race (1.25 mi), such as the Woodward, will be 121.70 s, rounded to two decimal places (with 'feet' hereafter abbreviated 'ft' and 'seconds' abbreviated 's').

The expected error limits of this prediction are then found using the standard error of estimate (SEE) value 0.3534. Multiplying SEE by three and then successively adding and subtracting the result from 121.70 gives you the 'three-sigma' boundary limits within which one can expect Buckpasser's predicted times to match actual times at ten furlongs.

The ±3 SEE range for this data is from (121.70 – 1.06) to (121.70 + 1.06), again rounding to two decimal places. These values are 120.64 and 122.76, respectively.

Figure 2 is the graph of Buckpasser's linear trend equation. The trend equation and COD are displayed near the upper right-hand corner of the graph. As in the preceding example, Buckpasser's slope of 107.91 means that, for an increase in x of one mile, the time value for $\hat{y}$ will increase by 107.91 s. You should verify this result using the graph and the equation for practice.

Figure 2

Buckpasser's Linear Trend for 1967 Races

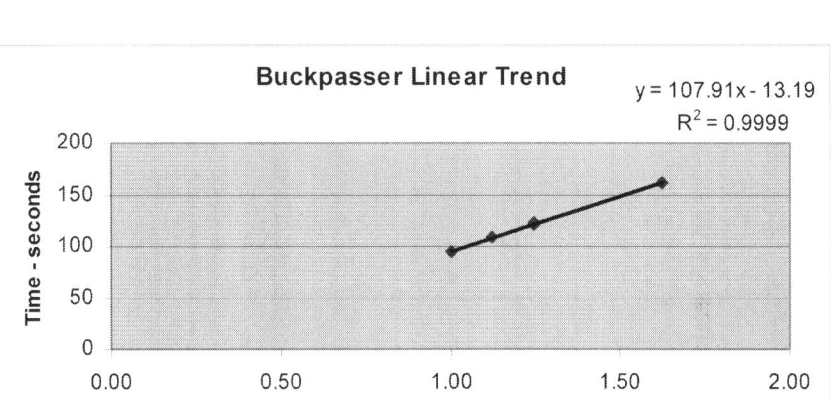

When LINEST is run for Damascus and Dr. Fager, their result-ing predicted mean times to run 1.25 miles are 121.81 s and 120.72 s, respectively.

Thus, based on this analysis, one would expect Dr. Fager to win slightly over Buckpasser and for Damascus to come in third, or to show.

The important conclusion of this example, however, differs. The *actual running* of the 1967 Woodward resulted in the following final times for the three horses – Damascus: 120.60 s, Buckpasser: 122.08 s and Dr. Fager: 122.15 s.

Damascus actually won the race by ten lengths over Buckpasser and by ten and one-half lengths over Dr. Fager.

Does this mean that such analyses are useless? No. It simply means one must always remember that *statistics only estimates* likely outcomes. Any estimate is always subject to error limits as given by the SEE. In this case, the following explanation for the race results clarifies much of the discrepancy between predicted and actual values.

The primary reason for Dr. Fager's relatively poor showing was that he was 'baited' into an early sprint-like duel with Damascus' stable-mate, Hedevar. This ploy worked mainly because Dr. Fager hated to let other horses lead him. By the time he reached about the final half mile of the race he had spent his energy and slowed dramatically.

In four total real-life matches, Dr. Fager actually had a two-two split in wins against Damascus. He was every inch Damascus' equal as a runner.

The z-score: An Important Comparison Factor

A theoretical z-score gives the relative performance level for a horse in any given race. It is calculated by *subtracting the horse's predicted average time*, from his linear trend analysis (LTA) for a given distance, *from* his time for a particular race of equal distance and then dividing the result by his LTA standard error of the mean (SEE).

The z-score formula is not given here. It can be found in any elementary statistics text. Excel also calculates it. The z-scores for the 1967 Woodward for Buckpasser, Damascus and Dr. Fager are: 1.09, -1.06, and 2.04, respectively.

Their z-scores are thus consistent with the race results. They indicate that Damascus ran near one standard deviation *below, or faster than,* his expected average time (thus, the negative value). Buckpasser ran about one standard deviation above, or slower than, his expected average time, and Dr. Fager showed the poorest overall relative performance, running a full two standard deviations above his expected average time. This explains his loss.

A Physical Analogy for a Race

It may help to visualize what statistics is trying to attain via mathematical analysis of sample data by imagining a horse race as a hockey puck lying on a flat, smooth surface and having various forces acting on it at random points around its circumference.

Imagine an arrow representing each force. The length and position of the arrows abstractly and symbolically represent the different relative influences each force has on the race's outcome. Longer arrows always imply stronger influences. Figure 3 aids this visualization.

Figure 3

A Graphic for Visualizing the Factors Influencing a Race

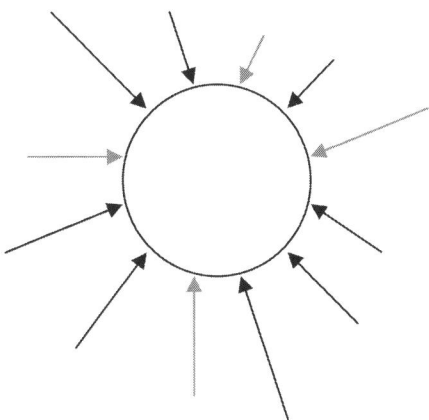

Figure 3 shows twelve arrows impinging on the circumference of the puck. Each represents some influence on the race's outcome. That outcome is expressed by the final direction the puck moves due to the predominant *resultant force* acting on it. Any set of such forces can always be reduced to a single resultant force acting at a specific angle.

It is not difficult to imagine at least twelve such factors that influence the result of a given race. One group might include, for example: track condition; length of race; weight carried (impost); post position; number of starters; rest time between races; gate conditions; overall health of the horse; climate factors; crowd noise; paddock incidents and track variant.

At the very least, it is nearly assured that the first seven listed conditions have some influence on the horse-jockey team, although their effects may not be quantifiable.

The four gray arrows in Figure 3 denote a random grouping of four factors that are assumed to affect the given horse most strongly on the particular day. We can imagine that such clusters of factors may affect a horse more at one time than at another and that they change from race to race. The analysis still remains valid.

If we calculate how many ways four of twelve factors may be randomly selected, we find that 495 unique groupings are possible. There is a formula for calculating this number that will not be given here. It is verbally stated as: *the number of combinations of n items taken r at a time.* It is symbolized: nCr or sometimes with the 'n' superscripted and the 'r' subscripted to the 'C'. In this case, r is four and n is twelve.

Many hand-held calculators compute nCr automatically with one button press once the total number of items and the group size are entered into memory.

It is quite reasonable to imagine four factors highly influencing a race outcome on a given day at a given time and place. This emphasizes why it is impossible to make a practical estimate of which horse in a group of, say, ten starters will win.

Obviously this situation makes betting the suspenseful pleasure that it is. If each race were nearly perfectly predictable, much of the sport's fun would be nullified.

Correlation and Statistics

To illustrate how the numerical effect (correlation) of random factors is calculated, data from Seabiscuit's past performance record are presented to examine the influence of several factors on his running times.

Fortunately, Seabiscuit ran enough races at a *given distance* on tracks having the *same rated surface condition* that this may be done with some degree of confidence. The data are from his 1936 racing season. He was then three years old.

Seabiscuit ran twenty-three total races in 1936. That is actually two races more than either Secretariat or Man o' War ran in their entire carriers of two years apiece.

Of those twenty-three races, eight were run at eight and a-half furlongs, or 1.0625 miles. Fortunately for analysis purposes, seven of those races were run on tracks rated fast, and three of the eight were run *on the same track* between Saturday, August 22 and Saturday, September 26. The running conditions for the three same-track races would logically be rated nearly identical, and so they would not be expected to bias the results.

Having this comparison allows us to see how much difference running equal distances *on the same track and under the same track condition* affects the correlations between the selected variables and the running time. It is not often that the small data samples available in thoroughbred racing comparisons give even this large a sample size wherein track conditions can be considered constant.

Table 2 lists the resultant correlations and related COD values for Seabiscuit. Recall that the COD is obtained by squaring the correlation coefficient, generally denoted 'r'. That is, if r = 0.50, then COD = r^2 = 0.25. The COD is actually the more important of the two numbers because it shows what percent of variation in the measure of interest is due to its affecting variable.

Table 2
Correlations and CODs of Run Time and Four
Important Factors: Seabiscuit, 1936

Results of Seven Races on Mixed Tracks			Three Races on Same Track		
Factor	Correlation, r	COD, r^2	Factor	Correlation, r	COD, r^2
Post Position	0.3290	0.1082	Post Position	0.9475	0.8978
Starters	-0.2885	0.0832	Starters	-0.2476	0.0613
Impost	0.2632	0.0693	Impost	0.6122	0.3748
Track Variant	0.4423	0.1956	Track Variant	0.7506	0.5634

Note the dramatic increase in both the correlation coefficient and the associated COD from the left half to the right half of Table 2 for three of the four factors. This occurs because the three races represented in the right half of Table 2 were all run on the same track, Detroit. It reminds us that 'fast' on one track does not generally equate to fast on another track.

This highlights a definite problem with data analysis in thoroughbred racing. Not only are sample sizes generally small, but there is also *insufficient duplication of race conditions* to allow reasonable certainty that bias has not affected the calculated results.

Recall that correlations have values between -1.00 and +1.00. A -1.00 correlation denotes a perfect *inverse relationship* between variables, while a +1.00 correlation denotes a perfect *direct relationship* between variables. In the former case one variable increases while the other decreases in step with it and vice versa for direct relationships.

To repeat, the *square of the correlation coefficient*, the COD, is really *the more important* of the two related numbers. The COD determines *what percent change* in the dependent variable (run time) is related to changes in the independent variable (distance).

In this regard, the negative correlation between running time and starters given in Table 2 implies that, for Seabiscuit's case, as his field size, or number of starters, increased, Seabiscuit's running times tended to decrease. That is, he ran better!

One would naturally expect the opposite. That is, the larger the field a given horse runs against, the more likely he would encounter interference and, hence, the longer running times one might expect.

This singular result in Table 2 emphasizes that one cannot always expect what otherwise seems common sense, especially when analyzing the small samples invariably found in thoroughbred data. It also makes one more cautious about interpreting correlations in general.

The final listed table value, Track Variant, describes how the average time for **all races on a given day at the same track and for the same distance** compares with the fastest time at that track for that distance in the past three years. If, for example, a track variant is listed in the performance line for the race as 05, it means that the daily average for all races at that distance was five fifths of a second (that is, one full second) longer than the lowest (fastest) time of the past three years.

The other table values are self-explanatory.

Limits Analysis

Limits Analysis is the final data technique used in this study to describe thoroughbred performance. This term simply means the plus-or-minus three-sigma (meaning three standard deviations) limits on either side of the mean or average for the distribution of a horse's run times *at a given distance.*

Essentially, ± 3 standard deviations includes the entire area under the normal curve, first given mathematically by Abraham DeMoivre in 1733.(4) It actually neglects the upper and lower 0.135 percent, but that fraction is irrelevant to analyzing racing data.

Figure 4 depicts Seabiscuit's run time distribution for his seven 8.5 f races on fast tracks only. The Shapiro-Wilk test shows it is normal. However, if his single 8.5 f race on a muddy track is included, the distribution is no longer normal. This highlights the sensitivity of the Shapiro-Wilk test, generally well regarded by statisticians.

Figure 4

Seabiscuit's Time Distribution for Seven 8.5 furlong Races, 1936

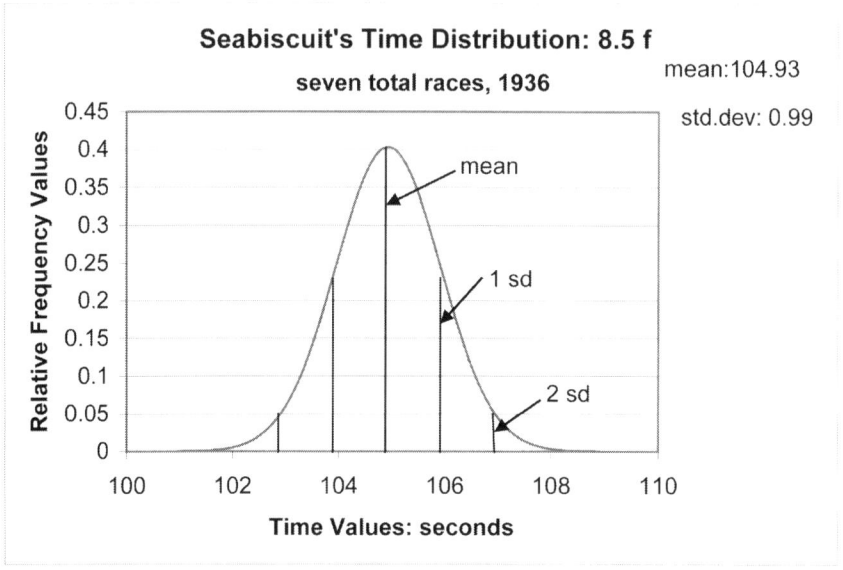

Since Seabiscuit's run times test as normally distributed, we can state several important things about what they represent. One feature of normality is especially useful when we wish to simulate many races between two or more horses. That is, for a normal distribution specific proportions of the area under the curve fall within one standard deviation unit of each other. Standard deviations are fully explained in Appendix A.

For the normal curve, exactly 34.13 percent of its area falls between the mean and one standard deviation either above or below the mean, since the curve is symmetrical around its vertical axis. Likewise, 13.59 percent of the area under the curve lies between plus one and plus two standard deviations above the mean, and similarly for that same interval below the mean.

Finally, 2.15 percent of the area under the curve lies between plus two and plus three standard deviations above the mean, and equivalently for that same interval below the mean.

The remaining area, beyond plus or minus three standard deviations from the mean, is approximately 0.27 percent of the total area under the curve. It may be ignored for the practical purpose of comparing thoroughbred race statistics.

These areas are highly important because they allow one to run unbiased simulations of hypothetical match races between any horses having normally, or near normally, distributed run times for a given distance.

If you know the average run times and standard deviations for, say, two horses at a given distance and under similar conditions of track surface and impost, you can use Excel to directly and reasonably calculate how many races out of one hundred, to use a convenient figure, Horse A would be expected to win at that distance from Horse B.

Two options are available in Excel for doing this. You can either use the NORMDIST function to compare the overlap areas of their run time distributions, or you can use the Random Number Generator (RND) to do the same thing. It is probably faster to do that latter.

Both methods are fully discussed in GHA, and the RND function is used in chapter seven to compare selected champion horses.

Regarding Seabiscuit's normal distribution for eight and one-half furlongs, we can also state that, with about 99.73 percent probability, his fastest expected time for that distance on fast tracks is 101.96 s while his slowest expected time is 107.90 s. He would not likely have run a faster or slower eight and one-half furlongs than these limits indicate, given that track condition and the errors inherent in small samples of size seven.

Looking Ahead

The only statistical methods this text uses which have not been discussed in this chapter are **data sorting** and the **t test** of sample means. They are much simpler to explain than are linear regression and limits analysis, and their exposition will be delayed until chapter four when the actual data to which they are applied is presented.

This concludes the overview of the main statistics used throughout this study. Colin's remarkable juvenile racing year is presented biographically in the following chapter.

Colin

And I saw when the Lamb opened one of the seals, and I heard,
as it were the noise of thunder, one of the four beasts saying,
Come and see. And I saw, and behold a white horse: and he
that sat on him had a bow; and a crown was given unto him:
and he went forth conquering, and to conquer -- Rev. 6:1-2[1]

CHAPTER 2

Colin

(1905 – 1932)

The final decade of the nineteenth century would bode unbelievably favorable for the twentieth regarding thoroughbred racing. In this respect, at least one lesser good counterbalanced the greater evil of President William McKinley's September 1901 assassination. His death would unfortunately prove a tragic harbinger of political carnage throughout the nascent century.

Despite its atrocities, however, life proceeds. And although McKinley, then forty-eight, probably did not know it, in the spring of 1891 the mare, Mannie Gray foaled a colt by Himyar at Hira Villa Stud near Lexington, Kentucky. In two years that colt's racing prowess would earn him the epithet 'The Black Whirlwind.' His more mundane name was Domino. In ten years, McKinley – Union Army brevet major, Ohio governor, congressman and United States president – would die, assassinated by Leon Czolgosz.

Domino raced unbeaten as a two-year-old, besting opponents nine consecutive times in his juvenile season. He capped his career with a final four-year-old season in 1895, a winning record of 19-2-1 in twenty-five races, and a lifetime earnings of $193,550 which remained unchallenged for twenty-seven years.

In 1898 he sired Commando out of Emma C. by Darebin. Commando eventually ran nine times in a two-year career and amassed a record of 7-2-0. He lost only the Matron Stakes, his final juvenile outing, by one-half length and his final career race, the Lawrence Realization, run on a muddy track, by two lengths.

And, as though to make amends for these *faux pas*, although obviously undreamed then, Commando sired a colt out of the British mare, Pastorella, at Hira Villa Stud in 1905 that became and remained one of the all-time darlings of American thoroughbred racing.

For reasons known only within the intricate workings of De Courcey Forbes' mind, the colt's name was chosen because a pastoral poem, 'Poor Colin,' written by English poet laureate Nicholas Rowe, seemed to appropriately link the dam's name, Pastorella, to that of the colt's trainer, James G. Rowe Sr. Forbes was a personal friend of the colt's owner, James R. Keene.

Thus, a brown colt having three white stockings, a stripe and a snip on his face, was foaled at Castleton Stud near Lexington, Kentucky. And he brought glory to all concerned by racing – undefeated in two seasons – under the unassuming name, Colin.

Colin was bred and raced by James R. Keene, a Londoner turned American who eventually made and lost fortunes on Wall Street, himself earning the epithet 'The Silver Fox of Wall Street.' Mr. Keene was not keen, however, about his colt's enlarged hock.

Nonetheless, Mr. Rowe, known as a true horseman, showered his well-known solicitations for his charges upon Colin and put him in racing form. The results follow.

The Maiden Race

Colin began his juvenile season on Wednesday, May 29, 1907 in a five-furlong (five eights of a mile) maiden special weights race, the second race slated for the day at Belmont Park. Twenty-two other entrants stood between him and victory. This huge field was apparently inconsequential to Colin since he won on a track rated good in 1:01 (61.0 s) flat. He led that race at each of the call points, having started in post position number ten and carrying 110 pounds. Colin's final winning margin was two lengths.

With but a laudatory comparison intended, Secretariat ran a five-furlong warm up at age three in 0:57.60 s at Woodbine track in Ontario, Canada in November 1973. It was in preparation for his final career race, the Canadian International.

As for all races but one of his juvenile year, Walter Miller was Colin's jockey. Mr. Miller would eventually be inducted into the jockey hall of fame in 1955.

The National Stallion Stakes

Colin was next entered in the National Stallion Stakes, also held at Belmont Park, on Saturday, June 1, 1907. It was the third race on the docket, and he now held the number three post position.

He had only three days rest from his maiden. Nonetheless, he again led at all the call points, this time carrying the 122 pounds of Mr. Miller and tack through five furlongs on a fast-rated straight track.

He was 'never threatened,' as his comment line indicates, and won by three lengths in a new track record time of 58.00 s over five rivals.[2] Note the closeness of his time for this race to that of Secretariat's warm up. This should suggest something to those constantly harping about era differences – that older tracks weren't *a priori* slower!

A Muddy Eclipse Stakes

Now, just four days later, Colin faced the challenging Eclipse Stakes, again at Belmont Park. It was pouring rain on that Wednesday, June 5 day during race number three, a five and one-half furlong sprint on the straight but muddy track. In addition, Colin had bucked shins, and so was presumably not one-hundred percent physically.

He was still asked to run, nonetheless, and faced five other horses while carrying 125 pounds, his greatest impost to that point. He started from post position six, this being his only juvenile race in which he was not ridden by Walter Miller.

Somewhat remarkably, considering the bucked shins, muddy track, unfamiliar jockey and less favorable post position, Colin broke second from the gate but proceeded again to lead at the call points and – at the most important point – the wire.

He won by a head in 1:06.6, finishing 1.2 s off the track record. His comment line reads 'under pressure; gamely.' This seems understated, all factors being considered.

The track variant for that day for five and one-half furlong races was 07. This means that the average such race was run in seven-fifths of a second (1.40 s) slower than the past three-year's fastest time for the same distance and conditions. Colin's finish thus was 0.20 or one-fifth second faster than average for that day and for those conditions.

It was a strong showing of Colin's character, considering the rather unfavorable conditions attending the race.

The Great Trial Stakes

Colin's racing venue now shifted to Sheepshead Bay, New York. It was twenty-four days since the Eclipse Stakes, but Colin's impost, as is generally true for horses gaining in racing stature, was increased to 129 pounds. At least his old familiar rider, Walter Miller, would be up again and would stay with him for the duration of his juvenile season.

The Great Trial was a 25k ($25,000) stakes race, the most prestigious race in terms of purse that he had yet run. It was set for the third race of that Saturday, June 29 day, and Colin drew post position seven. Thirteen other runners challenged him for the prize, and the track was not in top shape, being rated slow at the start of the six-furlong run.

Colin's post position was number seven – a presumable improvement over his previous start.

He broke second from the barrier, a spring-loaded net that was then used – mechanical gates not having yet been developed. At that point he had not seriously begun to run.

Colin, in his typical style, accelerated rapidly, and he was second by a length at the quarter-mile call. This spurt was probably the first time Colin evidenced the trait of fast acceleration at will.

Just two races later, after his win in the Saratoga Special Stakes, Walter Miller noted that even when Colin was loafing along he could get into action faster than any horse he had seen when it was necessary and that it seemed he could go from that loafing gallop into full racing speed in one stride but that he didn't want to do more than needed.[3] Readers should heed this comment. A chestnut colt of the 1970s is immediately recalled.

This particular spurt, however, allowed Colin's lead in the Great Trial Stakes to equal one length at the half-mile call. His lead then widened to two lengths at the five-eighths call, and he retained that margin over Meelick at the finish. His time of 1:12.40 boosted his record to four-for-four.

And it earned his performance line the comment: "Mild restraint."

The Brighton Junior Stakes

Twenty-eight days passed. The six-furlong race at Brighten Beach, New York found Colin once again less than totally sound. He had a slight cough, although his swollen hock was showing signs of receding. Horses were regularly asked to produce more then than in today's races.

Be that as it may, Colin assumed post position number two carrying 127 pounds. Seven other entrants were in various stages of nervousness at the barrier when the net jerked upward, freed of its spring restraints.

The track was rated fast for this fourth race of Saturday, July 27. Colin again broke second from the barrier, but he lead by a half length at the quarter-mile. He never relinquished that lead, extending and holding it, at one and one-half lengths throughout the remainder of the race, even though his comment line – perhaps suggesting a closer contest – notes that he 'repelled the stretch challenge.'

His final time for the six furlongs was 1:12.2.

The Saratoga Special Stakes

When the time arrived for Colin's sixth start of his juvenile season, he was still coughing and not looking well. Despite the ill-boding signs, he was again asked to start.

It was now Saturday, August 10. Colin would carry 122 pounds in the third race at famed Saratoga Race Track in Saratoga Springs, New York.

As he assumed his number-two position at the barrier, Walter Miller undoubtedly felt solicitous over his mount's general condition.

By now, however, Colin's reputation was such that he faced only one opponent, a horse named Uncle that was previously unbeaten. However, this day would end that untarnished streak, although Uncle put up a good fight.

Colin broke second from behind the barrier but led by a head at the quarter-mile call. He remained a head up on Uncle until the half-mile marker, at which time he began kicking it up a notch and extending his lead to a full length at the five-eighths call and retaining that margin across the wire.

He finished the six furlongs in 1:12.00. It was this race that prompted Mr. Miller his jockey to give the assessment of Colin's acceleration previously cited.

Although nobody could estimate it then, Colin had now completed the first half of his juvenile racing season. He remained unbeaten. His respite would be brief. He would run again in four days.

The Grand Union Hotel Stakes

Wednesday, August 14, 1907 offered another fast track of six furlongs at Saratoga for the third race. Colin's cough had stopped. By now he had impressed aficionados sufficiently that The Thoroughbred Record noted that he had become as much of a public idol at Saratoga as at Brighton Beach and Sheepshead Bay and that his defeat would have been viewed as a public calamity.

Nascent fear mongers need not have worried. Colin won again, this time dispatching five rivals in the time of 1:13.00. He departed the barrier from his number three position running fourth. It would prove to be the worst position at the start of a race he would hold for the remainder of his first season.

Despite his leisurely start, he was in second by a head at both the quarter- and half-mile calls. By the five-eighths mark he was leading by a head and won going away by two lengths over Jim Gaffney and by another three over Ben Fleet.

His comment line simply states: 'Hard held.'

The Futurity Stakes

Colin's eighth juvenile race, his fifth straight six-furlong race on a fast surface, came at Sheepshead Bay, New York. It was his second time at that venue.

It was a packed house that Saturday, August 31, with an estimated 50,000 in attendance, and Colin was not about to disappoint. He put on a dazzling show, running the three-quarter miles on the straight track in 1:11.20 while carrying 125 pounds. It was a stakes record but fell three-fifths of a second behind the track record. He won by one and one-half lengths even while starting from the number five post position and being 'Blocked, as rider pleased,' according to his comment line.

If another comparison is now in order, let it be that the fastest six furlongs *ever* run in the Belmont is 1:09.80, just 1.40 s faster than Colin's effort. The colt in question was the three-year-old Secretariat. Many now called Colin 'master' of the situation.

The Flatbush Stakes

Master or not, Colin was given one week before again running. This would be his longest race to date, seven furlongs at Sheepshead Bay on Saturday, September 7. The track was listed as fast, and Colin was perhaps aided by the lighter impost of 120 pounds.

With such an 'advantage,' he easily dispatched the closest of six other competitors, Celt, by three lengths. Bar None this time finished third, another five lengths back.

Colin's time was 1:24.80 for this effort, seven furlongs being the longest distance classified as a sprint. His time equaled the track record. It was the third time in nine outings that Colin had either bettered or equaled track records. And yet his most impressive performance awaited as the Fates patiently threaded their spindles.

Had he been able to prognosticate, Bar None might have sympathized with Sham running against Secretariat. This was the fifth time he was entered against Colin, and the closest he came to this point was by finishing one and one-half lengths in arrears in the previous week's Futurity. He could now relax, for he and Colin would not meet again.

The Brighton Produce Stakes

Twenty-three days later, a most generous respite for him, Colin readied himself to run a muddy surface for six furlongs at Brighton Beach, New York, his second juvenile, and final career appearance, at that track.

Just three colts faced him, but one of these was the highly respected Fair Play. Colin was again assigned 125 pounds; he drew the number-one post position.

He broke first from the barrier, as he did in seven of his twelve juvenile starts, and was never headed. His leads at the quarter-, half- and five-eighths call points were one and a-half, four, and four lengths, respectively. He topped off this display winning on the splattering surface by five lengths over Fair Play with the latter a head up on the show horse, Royal Tourist.

His time of 1:12.60 was just four-fifths seconds off the track record. This performance elicited more praise from the Thoroughbred Record to the effect that the more one saw Colin, the firmer was one's conviction that he was the best horse ever bred or raced in America.

Although time has quite unjustifiably pushed Colin's name into the shadows behind such track darlings as Man o' War and Secretariat, it was obvious then that he was something extraordinary. Chapter four adduces support for this comment.

The Matron Stakes

Although the name might intimate this as a race for fillies, at the time it was not. It was restricted to colts and geldings. It was run at prestigious Belmont Park on the crisp early autumn Monday of October 7, 1907. Belmont's six-furlong surface was rated fast.

Chapter four explains why 'fast' at Belmont in 1907 was definitely slower than 'fast' at Belmont in 1919 when Man o' War first ran there. However, for ease of exposition now, that caveat should simply be noted.

Colin once again faced Fair Play plus Royal Tourist and one other colt. He lined up in post position three and accepted his 129-pound impost with his usual equanimity, apparently similar to how Miller, his rider, described his acceleration at will.

There is something about the truly great ones that apparently scoffs inwardly at such pathetic human contrivances as adding the piquancy called 'impost' to their spectacles.

Colin, after all, had shouldered the same impost in just his fourth juvenile start, the Great Trial Stakes of Saturday June 29, when he was less mature by more than three months. That is a significant age factor for a growing colt.

We might imagine Colin wishing to tease his rivals on that lovely October day, for although he started first from the barrier, he trailed the leader by four lengths at the quarter-mile call.

Somewhere between the quarter and half mile marks, however, Colin shifted gears and gained nine lengths by the half-mile call. He then led by five lengths. He remained four lengths ahead at the five-eighths mile and went on to win by three lengths over Fair Play and by seven lengths over Royal Tourist.

His time was 1:12.00 flat for the six furlongs. Although his finish was two full seconds slower than the track record, it should be noted that his comment line indicated "Easing up.' Hence, he remained true to rider Miller's assessment of his talents.

The Champagne Stakes

It was Wednesday, October 16. Autumn's colors were now even more poignantly brilliant around Belmont Park's track than for the Matron Stakes just nine days past.

We humans often like to think that nature senses times of import in our affairs and becomes a bit more prodigal with her beauty on such occasions. This was such a transition occasion, for it marked the close of Colin's first racing year, arguably the greatest yet produced by an American colt and possibly, the greatest ever produced.

One exception to that remark may justly be noted, and it concerns a magnificent bay colt named Sysonby who raced three years before Colin. Sysonby will be given due notice in chapter eight with four other "honorable mention" horses.

But the race this October day was set for seven furlongs on the straight course. It was the second and final time for the season that Colin faced the longest of the accepted sprint class races.

Only one other entrant, a filly named Stamina, dared to challenge him.

The track was rated fast. The colt and the filly assumed their post positions for the day's third race – Stamina on the rail and Colin on her right. He carried 122 pounds to Stamina's 119, a seemingly equitable impost assignment for the filly.

As though he knew he would not tolerate a blemish on his perfect record to date, Colin simply put on a show of acceleration that gave Stamina no chance.

He led by three lengths at the quarter call, by four at the half-mile, by five at five furlongs and by six as he crossed the finish. His time, 1:23.00 flat for seven furlongs was not only a new track record but a new American record for the distance on a straightaway. The Fates nodded approvingly and smiled, their spinning completed.

One may easily calculate Colin's average speed for the Champagne Stakes to be 55.66 ft/s and his average sustained race momentum as that speed multiplied by the impost he carried. Adding 1.80 pounds for the steel racing plates he wore to the weigh-in weight of 122 pounds (jockey plus tack) and then multiplying the resultant total weight of 123.80 pounds by his average speed gives 6891.04 momentum units.

This is an impressive number comparing very favorably with the momenta of champions like Man o' War and also with more modern horses. This point is further explained in chapter four.

Naturally, Colin was mobbed in the paddock by fans and The Thoroughbred Record abundantly gushed over his dominance. Colin had thus ended what was possibly the most brilliant juvenile racing season ever crafted by an American colt to that point.

Colin had amassed twelve wins in twelve starts. Neither Man o' War nor Secretariat achieved as much. Each had one blemish on his juvenile record.

Colin raced on tracks under conditions ranging from muddy to fast and had traveled distances from five to seven furlongs. He bore imposts ranging from 110 pounds (only in his maiden) to 129 pounds (twice). He raced with bucked shins, a swollen hock and a cough – and he always won.

Colin went on to race three times as a three-year-old. He won all three races and retired undefeated. He is one of only two horses to achieve that distinction among the top one hundred Thoroughbreds of the twentieth century, as ranked by The Blood-Horse, Inc. in 1999 (2). The filly Personal Ensign is the second and last to have achieved that honor, in 1988.

Since this book's purpose is to focus almost solely on the juvenile season, nothing further will be noted regarding Colin's second short racing season. Some pundits argue that he should not have run at all that second year of 1908, but he ran and won despite general infirmities that likely would have beaten other horses. Fortunately, common sense finally took hold of his stewards and overcame greed. Colin was retired.

Colin lived to age twenty-seven, a good lifespan for thoroughbreds. He died in 1932 and was interred at Belray Farm near Middleburg, Virginia. In 1956 Colin was inducted into the National Museum of Racing Hall of Fame.

The previously mentioned Blood-Horse Magazine ranking as fifteenth in the top one hundred Thoroughbreds of the twentieth century placed him in very elite company – between Buckpasser at fourteenth and Damascus at sixteenth.

Although this is indeed a prestigious placement, one justly wonders whether even this high a level is adequate, given Colin's accomplishments.

Colin, in fact, made such an impression on those who worked with him that his trainer, James G. Rowe Sr. is reputed to have once said that all he wanted for his epitaph was: 'He trained Colin.'

Perhaps Kent Hollingsworth wrote the most tellingly and succinctly on Colin's prowess in his book *The Great Ones*: "Great horses have been beaten by mischance, racing luck, injury and lesser horses running the race of their lives. None of these, however, took Colin. He was unbeatable". (5).

May you rest always in sublime peace, great Colin!

Man o' War

And when he had opened the second seal, I heard the second
beast say, Come and see. And there went out another horse that
was red: and power was given to him that sat thereon to take
peace from the earth, and that they should kill one another:
and there was given unto him a great sword. -- Rev. 6: 3-4

CHAPTER 3

Man o' War
(1917 – 1947)

World War I, the 'Great War,' was busy taking lives in Europe and in making heroes of those piloting the new airborne killing machines that dotted the skies of France – men like Manfred von Richthofen (the Red Baron) and his brother, Lothar, Oswald Boelcke, Ernst Udet and numerous other German 'aces.'

Incongruous as it seems, while some Americans were giving their lives to this cause, others were enjoying the 'Sport of Kings' back home.

By early spring of 1917 Colin was twelve years old and living peacefully ensconced at Belray Farm in Middleburg, Virginia, justly reaping the rewards of his stellar career.

Less than four hundred miles away, at a place called Nursery Stud near Lexington, Kentucky, financier August Belmont had arranged for his stallion Fair Play to meet and woo a mare who was an undistinguished runner but, so he presciently guessed, would prove a great dam of runners, Mahubah.

Her name was Arabian for "May good things be with you". And, issuing from Fair Play's and Mahubah's cooperation, more monetarily good things soon came to Mr. Belmont, increasing his already appreciable wealth.

For Mahubah's second foal, arriving just before midnight on Thursday, March 29, 1917, was a chestnut colt, sturdily built and resembling Fair Play – having a white star on his forehead and a white streak that took a slight angle rightward as it ran down the ridge of his nose.

The sire of this foal had lost four times to Colin, but came within a head of winning in Colin's probably ill-advised, final career race – the rain-soaked, fog-enshrouded Belmont of 1908.

Colin, by then, had simply suffered too much bodily wear and tear, and would have been done a favor by not having been run. He did run and then left the country for England, the intent being to run him more. But he simply gave too many signs of being ill fit for further racing and was retired to stud.

Not long after the foaling, Mr. Belmont's wife, Eleanor Robson Belmont, named this chestnut colt to symbolize her husband's recent commission as major in the Quartermaster Corps, a position he recently assumed because America was gearing up for war and would declare so against Germany scarcely more than a year hence.

She christened him 'Man o' War.' With hindsight always easy, it seems that the name was, at best, a misnomer. Perhaps it was a result of Mrs. Belmont's decidedly genteel concept of the 'war' her husband would face. After all, questions of his masculinity aside, being assigned as major in a distinctly non-combat unit should not qualify in any generally accepted interpretation of the term soldier.

Nonetheless, the colt grew strong and hungry to run – to have, it would seem, a disdain for allowing other horses to get or remain ahead of him. This chestnut foal with the foreboding moniker was destined to bring everlasting fame to himself, his breeder, owner, trainer, jockey – to everybody remotely associated with his racing career.

Indeed, even the gentle, self-deprecating and yet uncommon man who cared for him personally for twenty-seven years after he retired, Will Harbut his groom, is undoubtedly – and sadly – remembered only through his association with Man o' War.

As do all wars, the Great War finally subsided. Victories and defeats were tallied. Wounds and egos were conveniently assuaged. Debts and promises were collected, or neglected – in other words, the spoils were apportioned. Life returned to its new version of normalcy, except for the lucky or the famous but unlucky.

The great German aerial fighter, Baron Manfred von Richthofen, was mortally wounded, perhaps through an instance of rare personal misjudgment, on Sunday April 21, 1918. While flying over Morlancourt Ridge near the Somme River a single .303 caliber bullet severely damaged both his heart and lungs. He managed to land his Fokker FI safely, and to die in the cockpit, just north of the village of Vaux-sur-Somme. "Kaputt" (roughly translated, "It's over.") is said to have been his final earthly utterance. (6)

It was eleven days before his twenty-sixth birthday and just seven months before the conflict ended. But his immortality was now assured, although it remains uncertain how much the dead appreciate the posthumous immortality bequeathed by the living.

And so events moved on as they always must – amid all the myriad human affairs that would render minds numb, were a mere mortal able, from space but beyond time, to comprehend in a single glance history's complete tapestry being threaded by the Fates.

A Maiden Special Weights Race at Belmont

Twenty score and fourteen days beyond the Red Baron's demise in the fields of France, Friday, June 6, 1919 arrived at a place in New York State called Belmont Park.

Samuel D. and Elizabeth Dobson Riddle, owners of a colt facing his maiden outing, sat attentively in the Belmont stands that afternoon, awaiting the 5:10 p.m. starting time of the day's sixth race – a five-furlong sprint on a fast-rated, straight track.

Thus were the general circumstances under which their often recalcitrant young colt called Man o' War would launch a running career perhaps yet unequalled in racing's chronicles of notoriety and fame.

Fifty-nine seconds later, the five furlongs was history. So relatively easy was the win, that jockey John Loftus was standing straight up in the stirrups as his red horse crossed the finish line. His closest competitor, Retrieve, was six lengths back. It was the second-fastest five furlongs run that spring at Belmont, just two-fifths of a second behind Dominique's 0:58.60.

The starter, Marshall (Mars) Cassidy later told jockey Loftus that the other colts were either bums or he had the fastest horse that ever lived. Cassidy added that Man o' War had broken so fast from the barrier, a spring-loaded net then used for aligning horses before the start of races, that he nearly recalled them. (7)

Cassidy, for whatever instinct, did not recall the horses, and Man o' War's nascent legend began.

The Keene Memorial Stakes

Just three days elapsed since Man o' War's maiden win. He was now again at Belmont, this time entered in a five and one-half-furlong run which, unfortunately that day, would be on a slow but straight track, the air being laden with a sullen mist.

Five other challengers lined up at the barrier with him, Man o' War drawing the third post position in this the fourth race of the day. A horse named Hoodwink, of which more will be heard later, was also entered.

The start of the race and actually the first four and one-half furlongs of its length were obscured by fog. The horses did not emerge into view until about one furlong from the finish. At that point My Laddie was leading, Ralco was second and Man o' War was in third a length behind.

It looked as though Man o' War had already lost, but he was not yet in high gear. Just then Loftus asked him to go, and the powerful colt accelerated. When it was done, Man o' War had won by a full three lengths over On Watch who had by then passed the tiring My Laddie and Ralco.

The time was 1:05.60, some six and six-tenths seconds slower than the five furlongs of his maiden, this being the extra time it took Man o' War to run one-half furlong – 330 feet – farther.

The Riddles were $5,000 richer, that being a ten-fold increase in winnings from the $500 of his first start. All this was, however, somewhat unimportant to the wealthy Riddles, their real pleasure being in the pride of owning and watching Mar o' War.

It is easily calculated that Man o' War ran his five furlong maiden race at an average speed of 55.93 feet per second (hereafter abbreviated ft/s) and his second race, one half furlong longer and on a slow track, at 55.33 ft/s.

It is likely that, had he been somewhat pushed, he could have run both lengths at the same average speed. However, attempting simply to show off speed, termed being a 'whoop-de-do' rider in racing lingo, is not how jockeys generally stay in demand by owners or trainers.

This is a good time to comment that Belmont's surface had been treated the previous winter with the express purpose of making it fast. A detailed discussion about this fact is given in chapter four.

However, any comparisons between Man o' War and Colin, who ran at Belmont as a two-year-old in 1907, must account for this track alteration.

It is also appropriate to mention now that John Loftus worked with Man o' War to prepare him for leaving the barrier quickly. Loftus soon noticed that each starter generally showed a characteristic bodily motion that indicated they were about to release the barrier. He took advantage of this, combined with the fact that Man o' War also learned that the barrier – actually, similar to a volley ball net – would yield somewhat to him, thus allowing him to literally push under and through it. (7)

All this, naturally, became an advantage over other horses. Apparently starters did not seriously question this behavior, probably categorizing it as one of those actions that are "fair in love and war."

Given these facts, those who baldly state that the starting methods used in Man o' War's era penalized or disadvantaged him are totally unjustified – to be euphemistic.

The Youthful Stakes

Man o' War now rested twelve days until Saturday, June 21, the date for the Youthful Stakes held at Jamaica Track in Jamaica, New York, a track no longer extant.

This was another $5,000 race of five and one-half furlongs. The track's rating was good. Red's reputation (he was first given the honorific name 'Red.' It soon became 'Big Red') was growing quickly enough in racing circles, that only three additional entrants faced him.

His weight assignment (impost) now jumped five pounds over his previous two races – to 120 pounds. He thus was giving his rivals between 12 and 15 pounds. Such is generally the price of quality and promise in the field of thoroughbred racing.

The prevalent opinion then was that four pounds in a sprint (up to and including seven furlongs) handicapped a horse by a length (about eight feet). However, the term 'length' is ambiguous, sometimes considered as nine or ten feet – nose tip to tail base.

If this estimate were scientifically accurate, then Man o' War would be 'giving away' from three to nearly four lengths in this race.

Chapter four discusses how the theoretical definition of kinetic energy leads to an even greater estimate of winning margin than four lengths, given a twelve-pound impost disadvantage. In fact, it theoretically would be about twenty-three lengths.

Be all this theorizing as it may, the end result was that Man o' War won this outing by two and one-half lengths over On Watch who carried 108 pounds. The winning time was 1:06.60. Another $5,000 was deposited in the coffers of Samuel and Elizabeth Riddle, courtesy of their talented colt. Smiles prevailed in Man o' War's camp.

The Hudson Stakes

Louis Feustel, Man o' War's trainer, was now directed to enter his charge in the Hudson Stakes just two days later. Not much travel was involved, Aqueduct in Jamaica, New York, being just three miles from Jamaica where the Youthful was run.

This next test would revert to the distance of the maiden outing, five furlongs. It would be the final race under six furlongs of Man o' War's juvenile year.

The purse was lower, $3,400. However, the large chestnut-red horse didn't know or care about the money. He simply liked to run and was obviously talented at it, as his nearly outlandish imposts alone implied.

A new wrinkle was added, however, to this contest. He would now shoulder 130 pounds. It was the highest of his first-year imposts thus far, and it would also be assigned in his next five races. In only the final start, the tenth of his juvenile year, would he carry a lower impost – by three pounds. It is notable that no previous Hudson winner ever carried more than 125 pounds.

From his number-two post position he made another fast start on the other four contestants. It was so fast this time, in fact, that the comment line of his post-performance chart states that he 'broke through the barrier.' However, break through or no, the horses were not recalled, and his final time for the fast five-furlong track in that third race of a pleasant early summer's day was 1:01.60. He crossed the finish one and one-half lengths ahead of Violet Tip carrying twenty-one pounds less.

The Tremont Stakes

He would not run again until Saturday, July 5. However, that was only a twelve-day rest. He was scheduled to run the Great American Stakes on Saturday, June 28, but a bellyache the morning of the race prevented it. The pain probably resulted from his exceptional appetite; nonetheless, he was scratched from the Great American Stakes.

It should also be noted that, to that point, he had gained 130 pounds above his weight upon leaving Glen Riddle to begin his career. This fact provides yet another counter to those claiming he was undernourished or thus could have run even better.

Therefore, the Tremont Stakes, rather than the Great American Stakes, would next test this rising track star. He again would carry 130 pounds but this time for a $6,000 purse. Only two competitors, Ralco and Ace of Aces, would challenge him, but the outdoor temperature climbed to an uncomfortable eighty-nine degrees.

The third race that day was a six-furlong sprint at Aqueduct. After some two minutes to get three colts halfway settled at the barrier, John Loftus pretty much let Man o' War have his head, and the race was no contest.

Man o' War led by a length at each call point and at the finish, with

Ralco, carrying just 115 pounds, placing and Ace of Aces – another twenty lengths in arrears while carrying just 112 pounds – showing.

As in his previous race, Man o' War's impost made it the highest such burden ever carried by a Tremont winner.

Riddle and Feustel, owner and trainer, now decided he should rest. The next lucrative race was scheduled for Saratoga on August 2. It was the U. S. Hotel Stakes worth $9,800. To this point their big red horse had earned a tidy $16,175. This was just the beginning of the monetary largesse, however, that Man o' War bestowed upon the Riddles.

The United States Hotel Stakes

This race would mark the beginning race of the second half of Man o' War's juvenile season. There were five down and five to go, and he was looking more and more like a horse that simply could not lose.

This run potentially would be his most lucrative gift yet to Mr. and Mrs. Riddle, worth nearly $10,000.

Its running honored one of Saratoga's large hotels, and the purse was twice as high as any race the shiny chestnut colt had yet entered. As properly expected of such stakes, the competition was also judged proportionally stronger.

Three such top competitors included Upset, Bonnie May and Carmandale, all winners in their own right.

This was Man o' War's first time on the newly resurfaced Saratoga track, which had been purposefully worked the previous fall and winter to render it livelier.

And so he stepped up to his assigned number eight post slot, just two places inward toward the rail from the two outside horses that completed the field of ten.

The day was good, and the track was rated fast. It was the day's third race, and it was six furlongs – three-quarters of a mile.

Whether the good weather made the horses unusually frisky or not, various movements not to the starter's liking kept postponing the start for some six minutes. Man o' War would have to either drop behind or cut ahead of the seven horses to his left in order to gain good position near the rail. Loftus sat his mount a bit uneasily.

Fortunately for the colt and rider, they had worked on both dropping and cutting tactics and also anticipating when the barrier would lift. Man o' War actually went under the rising barrier as the other horses were still standing in anticipation, with the exception of Carmandale on his left. Carmandale's jockey had the foresight to closely watch Loftus' movements, and he was ready to go with him.

Even with the fast break of these two horses, the starter made no objections, and the entire field was allowed to run.

Man o' War never trailed. Carmandale was three lengths behind by the quarter call, and Man o' War held a four-length lead over Upset at the five-eighths point. He won by two lengths over Upset while easing the final one-sixteenth mile.

Carrying 130 pounds to Upset's 115, he left no doubt about which was the faster horse. His winning time was 1:12.40. It was two full seconds slower than the track record but it tied the stakes record. This was on a day when the average time for all races was three-fifths of a second slower than his.

The win was not without controversy. One newspaper noted that Mars Cassidy seemed to give John Loftus more liberty at the start than any other jockey. However, Mr. Cassidy had no obvious reason for allowing John Loftus liberties, if indeed they were allowed. And Loftus, it must be noted, had the intelligence to observe Mr. Cassidy's behavior at the barrier over many years of racing. He noticed how Cassidy generally flexed one knee just as he was about to press the button releasing the spring-constrained barrier (7). This was all Loftus needed for his tip-off.

The Sanford Memorial Stakes

In light of the previous discussion concerning complaints, it is instructive that Mars Cassidy called in sick for the Sanford Stakes, just eleven days later. Thus, Wednesday, August 13 arrived and a former but essentially retired starter was asked to fill in.

Mr. Charles Pettingill was at one time a prominent starter, but he had been engaged for some years as a placing judge – watching finishes closely from the stands and judging the winner in case of close calls.

Whether or not all this is truly meaningful to the outcome is history's secret.

The end result was that, seventy-one and two-fifths seconds after the Sanford Stakes finally began, Man o' War had suffered his first, and what would be his only, career defeat. And it was accomplished, ironically, by the horse named Upset that he had beaten handily less than two weeks previous.

Upset won by one-half length with Man o' War gaining fast but running out of distance. Six furlongs is a short span in which to correct for error, whatever its source. The horse finishing third of the seven-horse field was Golden Broom. He was owned by Sarah Jeffords, niece-in-law to Mr. Riddle. An entire and untold story attends that fact.

Naturally, impost could always be partially invoked as contributing to this loss. Man o' War carried 15 pounds more than Upset. This is also debatable since nobody knows the actual effect pounds of impost make per furlong of race. Correlations are contradictory in many facets of horse racing. However, since impost posed no obvious problem for him in the previous races, it did not become a major issue in this defeat.

Suffice it to say that if controversy had surrounded the possibility of his being favored by starters in previous outings, it was essentially redressed by the Fates in this effort.

Most accounts state that Man o' War was not even ready when the barrier lifted, having his backside actually turned toward the net.

This seems dubious due to the attention to detail that has already been noted about John Loftus and how he specifically worked with his mount on starting niceties. The situation could nearly cry for incompetence on the starter's part. However, even though he may have been a bit rusty at a task, it is also difficult to imagine that Mr. Pettingill did not see one horse of only seven actually facing backward when he lifted the barrier. The truth of this entire debate will never be known. Unfortunately, there are no known photographs – of this or any other race – of Man o' War actually at the barrier. (7)

Naturally, many people sought redress against Loftus for causing their favorite's loss. Everything from poor judgment to outright fixing of the race descended on the – until then - scrupulously clean rider. For a jockey known to prepare assiduously to begin cheating at this stage in his career also seems highly suspect, if not ludicrous.

Sadly, although Mr. Riddle protested his continued respect for his rider, as did the trainer Fuestel, John Loftus would not be chosen to guide Man o' War in his next and final racing season. A new jockey, Clarence Kummer, would be up.

Time, however, marches on. One old saying has it that there is no rest for the wicked. If Mr. John Loftus qualified for this epithet, he none-theless would be astride Man o' War in another ten days for the third race at Saratoga. Neither man nor steed received much rest, regardless of either's degree of inward purity.

The Grand Union Hotel Stakes

On Saturday, August 23, with a ten-horse field milling at the barrier, Mars Cassidy was once again the starter. Man o' War was posted at number two position for the day's third race. The track was rated fast, and the distance was six furlongs, a number that would remain constant for the remainder of Man o' War's juvenile year.

He again shouldered 130 pounds while six of the remaining nine entrants bore from 112 to 115. Only Blazes, winner of his last three sprints, carried 122 pounds while Upset, as a dubious reward for upsetting Man o' War, now carried 125 pounds.

The runners were not released until some five minutes later than intended, courtesy of the fidgetiness of Evergay and Hasten On, the latter creating a kind of ironic mockery of his name for this event.

As the barrier finally rose, Man o' War broke a leisurely third. From there on, however, it was his race. He led by margins of a head for the first quarter, three lengths at the half mile and the same at five-eighths. By the quarter pole Upset was trying his best to overtake him, but that effort was in vain.

So confident was he of winning that John Loftus began pulling back on the reins with about a furlong remaining. Man o' War crossed the finish while easing the final sixteenth in the stakes record, but not the track record, time of 1:12.00 flat. Upset was second a length back.

True to fickle human nature, at least one writer now praised John Loftus's riding – calling him a great jockey who had to stand in the irons near the finish and pull on his mount's reins to make the colt shorten stride. It is nothing short of astounding how a man can be a bum one day and a hero the next in our society.

The Hopeful Stakes

One week later, again at Saratoga, eight horses entered the Hopeful Stakes.

On Saturday, August 30, Man o' War and seven other thoroughbreds lined up for a race bearing the highest potential purse thus far in their juvenile careers – $30,000.

The distance this time was six furlongs. It was race number three for the day – a very hot and humid day with a foreboding sky.

Before they got under way – and beat the threat of rain – the weather intervened. Threat became reality, and they waited a full twelve minutes in a downpour. Man o' War chose to entertain the crowd by impatiently breaking through the barrier four times.

Cassidy finally let them run in the middle of the deluge. Most spectators would later say that the rain was so heavy they couldn't see much of anything. However, they did see a big red colt cross the finish line four lengths ahead of Cleopatra who carried eighteen pounds less. Even through weather-dimmed vision there was no mistaking him.

His time was 1:13.00. It was his slowest time for the distance and equaled his time for the Tremont Stakes.

Although it was a rather trudging romp through the soggy dirt, one New York paper called him one of the best two-year-olds that ever ran on this continent.

Thus did the season close that year at Saratoga's track.

The Futurity Stakes

Saturday, September 13, 1919 at Belmont Park would witness the final race of Man o' War's juvenile campaign.

The stands were jammed with some thirty-thousand spectators. John Loftus' mother, Margaret O'Dowd Loftus, had come to see her now famous son and the more famous horse he rode. (7) It was good that she managed this first and only look at the two together, for it was to be John Loftus' final up on Man o' War.

The actual purse was $26,650 to the winner. The contest was scheduled as the third event of the day. The ten entrants reached the barrier at 3:46 p.m.

Man o' War flirted briefly with his assigned number eight position but was apparently dissatisfied or agitated, for he would not settle in, insisting to fool around with dashes back and forth across the track, excursions to the front of and then behind the barrier, inside and outside the rails – generally making his jockey and all concerned quite anxious.

Finally the horses all settled long enough for Cassidy to let them go, and the entire group apparently departed in a fairly even line, according to reports.

Johnny Loftus, sadly, did not know that he was riding the spectacular red colt for his final time. Humans are often cruel in their laxity, unconcern and neglect.

Man o' War left the barrier in the number two position. By the time he reached the first quarter mile call he was third. The Belmont Park track, however, was so huge that most onlookers only saw the horses at first as specks. Furthermore, nobody was positioned along the track for the early going so that even the Daily Racing Form did not chart the initial quarter mile. Thus, no time exists in the records for this point in the race.

However, by a half mile Man o' War led John P. Greer by one-half length and at the finish by two and a half. Interestingly, John Loftus did what Ron Turcotte did as Secretariat approached the finish of the 1973 Belmont – looked behind briefly to see just how far ahead he was. In that later race, the glance covered 31 lengths.

The ending comment line for the magnificent chestnut colt's first year of racing stated laconically and elegantly: "Won easing up."

Man o' War's time was 1:11.60. It was a full three seconds slower than the then current track record, but it was the fastest Futurity since the race had moved, first from Sheepshead Bay where it was held before 1910 and, last, from Saratoga to Belmont Park in 1915. (8)

The great two-year-old would now rest. He would not run again until the first race of his sophomore, or three-year-old season – The Preakness Stakes at Pimlico Race Track (Old Hilltop) in Baltimore, Maryland.

He would not, unfortunately, be entered in the Kentucky Derby – for a complex series of supposed reasons that do not always seem consistent. Thus, he would never have a chance at the now-coveted Triple Crown, although he undoubtedly would have won and would have been granted it after-the-fact, as were Sir Barton and Gallant Fox.

In fact, Man o' War's linear trend analysis as a three-year-old predicts he would have run a typical ten-furlong race in 123.00 s. Paul Jones actually won the 1920 Kentucky Derby in a time of 129.00 s. Thus, all other factors having remained constant, Man o' War could possibly have won the Kentucky Derby by about a six-second margin.

Thus, the great red thoroughbred – foaled, reared and trained in Kentucky – would never race in the Commonwealth. That is another story, but it must stand in bold relief as one of the supreme ironies of thoroughbred racing.

For the final sixteen years of his life, Man o' War enjoyed himself at Samuel Riddle's Faraway Farm several miles from Lexington, Kentucky. There he became friends with a man who certainly had one of the great and loving souls ever placed upon an often uncaring earth – Will Harbut.

When Mr. Harbut died of a heart attack, Man o' War soon followed. He ended his stay on earth at age thirty – on Saturday, November 1,

1947. His funeral was broadcast nationally over radio. Fittingly, in one major Christian church, it was All Saints Day.

Among Man o' War's many honors are: Champion 2yo Colt, 1919; Champion 3yo Colt, 1920; Thoroughbred Racing Hall of Fame, 1957.

He was first interred at Faraway Farm. About thirty years later his remains were moved to the Kentucky Horse Park at Lexington, Kentucky. An imposing sculpture of him, completed several years after his death by Herbert Haseltine, was also moved and rests upon his grave.

Now it is appropriate for an informal comparison, with no intent of making final judgments about greatness, between Colin and Man o' War. Let it merely serve as a guide for future, brave souls who wish to explore statistics in an unbiased manner.

This comparison is simply intended to pave the wave, to illustrate techniques if you will, for those who insist upon a strict comparative evaluation of these or any other thoroughbred horses.

With that intent, it suggests statistical methods which, if used objectively, can help sort truth from conjecture regarding thoroughbred greatness. These methods do not, and cannot, offer a final "carved-in-granite" conclusion. Such is the nature of statistics.

As stated in GHA, only God knows the true greatness of the creatures he metaphorically summoned from the South Wind those countless eons past. And although it is now generally conceded by scientists that God does play dice – thus approving of statistics a priori – with the universe, He does not always tell us what He rolls.

A really naked spirit cannot assume that the world is thoroughly intelligible. There may be surds, there may be hard facts, there may be dark abysses before which intelligence must be silent, for fear of going mad. -- George Santayana

C H A P T E R 4

Colin and Man o' War: Combined Performance Review

This chapter presents an overview of the basic statistical methods used to analyze thoroughbred racing data. The past performance data of both Colin and Man o' War are viewed from three levels: data ranking, linear trend analysis and limits analysis.

The bases for these statistical methods were stated in Chapter 1 for readers unfamiliar with them. Two additional methods, briefly detailed in this chapter, are easier to explain than the previous techniques, and they will be discussed as they are introduced. These methods are: analysis of variance and the t test.

Using the term 'combined performance review' in the chapter heading is intended to alert readers to the idea that the chapter *suggests* how to further structure objective comparisons of thoroughbred data, if so desired.

The intent herein is not to reach definitive conclusions that one horse is better than another, but in showing how data may profitably and appropriately be compared, given the nature of small samples, before reasonably objective comments regarding thoroughbred performance are possible.

No implication is made herein that these are the only ways to compare such data.

Performance Ranking Indicators

We begin by listing a set of parameters that were selected as important to use for making judgments about thoroughbred performance. They are 'sort' parameters.

It must be noted, at least as a reminder if for no further reason, that Colin raced twelve times during his juvenile season of 1907 and Man o' War raced ten times during his equivalent season in 1919. Chapters 2 and 3 summarized each of the individual performances for each horse.

Both of these data sets, of sizes twelve and ten respectively, are deemed small for statistical analysis purposes, whether considered as populations *or* as samples, because each has well below 30 values.

As such, they invite premature conclusions and are subject to inaccuracy – unless proper caution is taken.

It bears repeated emphasis that one ***cannot use statistics to prove*** one horse is better than or greater than another. Even with large sample sizes, generally considered above 30 values, one cannot justly make such statements.

All one does in proper statistical evaluations is state either the ***acceptance or rejection*** of a pre-test hypothesis, termed the ***null hypothesis***. The null hypothesis is generally indicated by H_0. The null hypothesis is just a statement comparing two items.

The null hypothesis basically establishes the conditions under which one should accept or reject a conclusion such as – the difference observed between the means of two samples, for instance the mean running times for six furlongs – is or is not significant at some given confidence level, typically 0.05.

If the obtained difference is considered **significant**, generally with probability no more than five percent, of being in error, then ***the likelihood that the two samples could represent the same population,*** or populations having equal means, is low.

This **may or may not** imply, depending on other factors, that, for example, one of two horses being compared ran consistently better than another for six furlongs. That is the catch-22 of statistical analyses. Common sense must prevail in deciding such questions.

While such a conclusion might lead some to consider that this proves nothing of value, it should highlight *why purely subjective statements about the quality of one horse versus another are truly pointless and unscientific*. For if an objective mathematical analysis is subject to this restriction, all the more so are subjective utterances – often based on nothing more than one horse looking prettier! This same basic caveat is made in any competent statistics text, but it is often overlooked or ignored.

This warning having been given, we now examine some indicators culled from the past-performance data of Colin and Man o' War for their juvenile seasons only.

This study was generally restricted to the juvenile seasons of the four legendary thoroughbreds mainly because it clarifies issues that otherwise could easily be misconstrued. Individual thoroughbreds mature so differently that proper comparisons cannot be readily done by mixing the data from two or more racing seasons.

It is highly instructive, nonetheless, to determine just how many pertinent 'facts' concerning their performances might be gleaned from the sparse data available for each of their juvenile racing years alone. The results may prove surprising.

The Selected Ranking Factors

A list of factors, in bold face, follows. These factors were chosen to give a comprehensive overview of Colin's and Man o' War's running performances. A brief explanation accompanies some of these items for those cases where the meaning of the factor itself may not be intuitively obvious. Some are obvious without comment.

Thirteen factors were deemed relatively exhaustive of truly meaningful parameters that indicate excellence of juvenile racing ability. The reader may or may not agree on the exhaustiveness of this list, but each person has his or her own opinion in such matters. The list items are, at minimum, important racing parameters.

Overall Career Racing Records for Juvenile Year

Colin: 12: 12-0-0
Man o' War: 10: 9-1-0

Fastest Average Speed in a Race

Colin: 56.90 ft/s; 6/1/1907; 5f; fast track; 122 lb. impost
Man o' War: 55.93 ft/s; 6/6/1919; 5f; fast track; 115 lb. impost

Highest Momentum (impost x speed) Generated

Colin: 7095 units; 10/7/1907; 6f; fast track; 129 lb. impost
Man o' War: 7223 units; 8/13/1919; 6f; fast track; 130 lb. impost

Explanation: Momentum was already discussed regarding how it is a more inclusive performance indicator than is speed alone. Momentum is calculated simply by multiplying the horse's average speed for a race in feet per second by his impost in pounds. As such, it indicates an energy that the horse was capable of sustaining - the actual units being in *pound-feet per second*, but simply called *units* herein since only the numerical value is of interest. Kinetic energy may also be used for this indicator, but it is slightly more awkward to calculate and yields no greater information, still being the energy of motion generated by the horse. Pounds, vice mass, are used for simplification and only alter results by a factor of 32.2.

Greatest Action (momentum x distance) Generated

Colin: 5942 units; 10/16/1907; 7f; fast track; 122 lb. impost
Man o' War: 5417 units; 8/13/1919; 6f; fast track; 130 lb. impost

Explanation: When momentum, as defined above, is multiplied by the distance, in feet, of the entire race, it gives a slightly better perspective or different feeling for how given horses sustained their energy of motion over that race. This number naturally varies for different distances and imposts, depending on the horse. Its units, fully expressed, would be pound-feet squared per second (lb-ft^2/s) since the distance unit is multiplied by the pound-feet per second unit of momentum. However, merely stating units instead of actual lb-ft^2/s is sufficient for this type of data.

Average Weight Carried (impost) for All Races

Colin: 123.58 lbs.
Man o' War: 125.70 lbs.

Average Momentum for All Races

Colin: 6793 units
Man o' War: 6891 units

Average Action for All Races

Colin: 5064 units
Man o' War: 4920 units

Average Winning Margin (lengths) for All Races

Colin: 2.51
Man o' War: 2.30

Most Races at a Common Distance

Colin: 7 (of 12) at 6f
Man o' War: 6 (of 10) at 6f

Average Size of Field per Race

Colin: 7.5
Man o' War: 7.0

Average Post Position

Colin: 4.2
Man o' War: 4.5

Average Performance Figure

Colin: 2.92
Man o' War: 2.00

Explanation: For this study, the Performance Figure was defined as how many fifths of a second the given horse's *Speed Rating* for each race was either better or worse than the average *Track Variant* for all races at the same distance on that day for that track.

For example: suppose a given horse achieved a **Speed Rating** of 87 for a given race, (meaning that his time was 100 – 87 or 13 fifths of a second (2.6 s) slower than the track record *for the previous three years*, with 100 defined as the track record), and the **Track Variant** (how many fifths of a second slower than the track record the *average of all* races run that day) was 17 (3.4 s), or 100 – 83. Then the given horse's Performance Figure was *four fifths of a second better for that race* than the average at the track for all races run at that distance and on that day. Thus, the horse's Performance Figure was 87 – 83, or 4.0.

The above Performance Figures show that Colin averaged 2.92 fifths of a second (0.584 s) faster than the average winning horse, on the given day, for all his races. Likewise, Man o' War averaged 2.00 fifths of a second (0.400 s) faster than average winning horse for all his races.

Recall that one-fifth of a second is 0.20 s.

Average Track Record Comparison Number

Colin: -3.83
Man o' War: -11.30

Explanation: This number was chosen to represent simply how many fifths of a second, on average, the horses either broke or missed the track record for all their races. From the above, Colin averaged nearly four-fifths of a second *slower* per race than the existing track record, and Man o' War averaged a little more than eleven-fifths of a second *slower* than the existing track record per race. In other words, this would have given Colin an average Speed Rating of 100 – 3.83 = 96.17 and Man o'

War an average Speed Rating of 100 – 11.30 = 88.7, if Speed Ratings were actually expressed in decimal format.

If one sorted and ranked the above results and then assigned one point for the better score and zero points for the lesser score in twelve of the thirteen categories (number of common-distance races not counted), then Colin's point total would be 8 and Man o' War's 4. For what it's worth, that is the result of this particular rank comparison.

Linear Trend Analysis Results

Two related linear trends for both Colin and Man o' War are now examined. After this preliminary introduction, a brief overview of Sysonby's and Secretariat's two-year-old season linear trend is introduced for contrast. Factors detailed then will indicate why it is inappropriate to include the latter two horses in the same juvenile category with Colin and Man o' War.

Colin and Man o' War: Linear Trends for all Juvenile Races

The basics of computing and interpreting linear trends were described in chapter 1; thus, the results are all that need be presented now. All values are rounded to two decimal places except for the coefficient of determination, R^2.

Colin: $\hat{y} = 97.01x - 0.68$; $R^2 = 0.9856$, standard error = 0.95.

Man o' War: $\hat{y} = 95.61 + 0.49$; $R^2 = 0.9723$, standard error = 0.90

When these linear trend equations are used to predict times for the standard distances that either Colin or Man o' War would likely run, the following results are obtained, with distances in fractional miles and running times in seconds:

Colin:	Miles: 0.625,	0.6875,	0.75,	0.875
	Times: 59.95,	66.01,	72.07,	84.20
Man o' War:	Miles: 0.625,	0.6875,	0.75,	0.875
	Times: 60.24,	66.22,	72.19,	84.14

These data indicate, using the best predicted linear trend values, that Colin was slightly faster than Man o' War at the first three of the four standard distances, whereas Man o' War was faster, on average, at the longest of the juvenile distances either horse raced in common. Recall that Man o' War's six longest-distance juvenile runs were all six furlongs, or 0.75 miles. He did not run seven furlongs as a juvenile.

The differences in Colin's favor were: 0.29 s at five furlongs, 0.21 s at five and one-half furlongs and 0.12 s at six furlongs.

At seven furlongs, Man o' War's linear trend predicts him to be faster than Colin by 0.06 s. However, as just noted, Man o' War *never actually ran* seven furlongs as a juvenile. Thus, using his linear trend for this distance could produce greater estimation error than for Colin's case. This is one disadvantage of such analyses.

Further Considerations

A complication arises now due to facts regarding the surfaces on which the two horses ran.

It is well documented by Ours (7) that both the Saratoga and Belmont Park tracks were improved shortly *before* Man o' War ran his maiden race at Belmont Park.

Both tracks were resurfaced for the express purpose of making them faster. The work was completed in August 1918 for Saratoga. It was begun the following year and completed by mid May of 1919 at Belmont Park.

Ours documents that, shortly after these modifications, records began being broken regularly at both tracks. In fact, Belmont Park was considered fast enough by then to earn the nickname, 'the rubber track.'

Man o' War ran his maiden race at Belmont Park on Friday, June 6, 1919, as noted in chapter 3. Thus, he presumably had a time advantage over Colin due to Belmont Park's improved surface, and this must be considered in strict comparisons since it is the salient factor which differs between the two horses, considering the common general 'era' in which each ran. They were separated by only twelve years.

Given the above facts, the American Racing Manual 2005 (8) was used to compare the pre-1919 running times for the Saratoga and Belmont Park tracks – and also Sheepshead Bay times – with the *post-1919* Belmont Park running times.

To obtain adequate yet reasonably manageable data, annual running times were compared using data for the Futurity, a six-furlong race, for the years 1902 through 1924. Between 1902 and 1909 this race was run at Sheepshead Bay in New York. For 1910, 1913 and 1914 it was run at Saratoga, and from 1914 through 1924 it was run at Belmont Park. It was not run in 1911 and 1912. Its distance varied between 1925 and 1993. Therefore, data from 1925 onward cannot be included in the current comparison. However, enough years (23) are included to render this comparison meaningful.

Colin ran his Futurity at Sheepshead Bay in 1907. He carried 125 pounds, and his winning time was 71.20 s. Man o' War ran the Futurity at Belmont in 1919 carrying 127 pounds. His winning time was 71.60 s. Thus, Colin actually ran his Sheepshead Bay six furlongs in 0.40 s less. This will prove interesting considering what follows.

In fact, in four of the five years immediately following Man o' War's race, four different horses bested his time by anywhere from 0.20 s to 1.20 s. Few Man o' War devotees ever mention this, but – in all honesty – it is a matter of record.

One can perform pair-wise t tests between the tracks to determine whether significant differences exist among them. Six such comparisons are possible. A variant t test is used which must *follow* an analysis of variance (ANOVA) or risk false results. An ANOVA allows grouping and comparing the four means together. See Appendix B.

A single-factor (track effect) ANOVA is used. Excel provides the test. It is accessed using the menu sequence: *Tools, Data Analysis, ANOVA: Single Factor.* Using the dialog box provided, the run times for the tracks are entered from their respective spreadsheet columns. The ANOVA tests the null hypothesis H_0 that the mean times under four track conditions are equal against the alternative hypothesis H_1 that they are not.

It uses an F ratio and makes the test at the 0.05 significance level, or as directed. See Schmuller (9) for a good explanation of the single-factor

ANOVA. Only the result is given here – namely, that the four means differ at the 0.007 level. This level is highly significant, and thus H_0 is rejected. This result then allows using the variant t test given by the formula: $t = (\bar{x}_1 - \bar{x}_2)/\text{SQRT} [MS_w*((1/n_1) + (1/n_2))]$, where $\bar{x}_1$ and $\bar{x}_2$ and n_1 and n_2 are the respective means and sample sizes for the given track comparisons, and MS_w is the mean square within groups output by the ANOVA – 1.382 for this case.

The post-ANOVA t results and their significance levels for the six comparisons are: 1. Sheepshead Bay/Pre-improved Belmont: t = -0.417; sig. = 0.341; 2. Sheepshead Bay/Post-improved Belmont: t = 1.685; sig. = 0.056; 3. Sheepshead Bay/Saratoga: t = - 2.973; sig. = 0.004; 4. Saratoga/ Pre-improved Belmont: t = 2.305; sig. = 0.017; 5. Saratoga/Post-improved Belmont: t = 4.138; sig. = 0.0003; 6. Pre-/Post-improved Belmont: t = 1.805; sig. = 0.045.

Thus, t comparisons 3 through 6 are significant while 1 is not and 2 is marginal.

When one compares the running times for the Futurity at Belmont Park for the four years *previous to* the track improvement with the first six years *after* the improvement, the *t test* (explained later in this chapter) indicates that they differ significantly at the 0.045 level. This significance level means that there are only about four chances in one hundred (hence, the 0.045 value) that these two samples do not differ significantly.

As any basic statistics text confirms, statisticians generally consider a significance level of 0.05 or below sufficient to establish that two samples differ significantly from one another. Since 0.045 is less than 0.05, one must conclude that the two samples differ significantly. Another way to say this is that, if the two samples *were* drawn at random *from the same population*, or from populations having equal means, one *would not expect* a difference between their means as great as the one obtained.

This result implies that it is possible Man o' War had a running advantage for the year he ran at Belmont Park, as opposed to horses running there before the track improvement. It does not and cannot, however, state exactly what caused the difference.

Comparison with Pre-Improved Belmont Track

To make this comparison more meaningful, the running times at Sheepshead Bay centered around the year Colin ran (1907) were first compared via the t test (which is simply an algebraic comparison between sample means) with the *pre-improvement* times at Belmont Park before 1919.

When this was done, the test showed that these two sets of times did not differ significantly, the result being significant at the 0.341 level. This means that the result could be due simply to the randomness of sampling error – rather than to a real difference between the sample means – roughly thirty-four percent of the time.

This result lends enhanced meaning to a test of run time means for pre- and post-improved Belmont Park. For if Sheepshead Bay and pre-improved Belmont Park do not differ significantly, then a significant difference between pre- and post-improved Belmont implies that Sheepshead and post-improved Belmont also differ significantly.

Comparison with Post-Improved Belmont Track

The end result is that the pre- and post-improved Belmont tracks times do differ at the 0.045 level, and this is considered significant. Thus, as alluded to above, since Sheepshead Bay times are essentially equivalent to those of the pre-improved Belmont Park times, and pre-improved Belmont Park tests significantly different from post-improved Belmont Park, the conclusion *must be* that Sheepshead Bay times also *differ significantly* from post-improved Belmont Park times.

We are fairly safe, therefore, in stating that Man o' War had a time advantage over Colin due to the improved track condition – or some other unexplained factor – at Belmont Park when he ran his maiden race. We cannot state the exact time advantage.

The average running time for the Futurity at Belmont Park for the six-year sequence beginning with Man o' War's running in 1919 and ending in 1924, was 71.23s. The average running time for the Futurity at Sheepshead Bay for the eight years between 1902 and 1909, Colin's range of years, was 72.30 s. The difference is 1.07 s.

Since we've shown that a likely significant difference exists, it is important to determine how much time should reasonably be subtracted from each of the Sheepshead Bay times so that they definitely show no significant difference relative to the post-improved Belmont Park times. This adjustment seems only fair. It can be accomplished using the post-ANOVA t test in a kind of inverse application from its normal use.

Explanation of the t Test

The t test is a statistical device for comparing the means of two samples to determine whether they differ significantly. It is particularly important for comparing thoroughbred racing data, especially where questions arise concerning presumed era effects.

For this example and explanation, actual data from the Futurity six-furlong race for three separate time periods are compared using the t test *after* single-factor ANOVA.

Recall that, between 1902 and 1909, the Futurity was run at Sheepshead Bay in New York. In 1919 Man o' War ran this race at Belmont Park and won by two and one-half lengths over John P. Greer. It was Man o' War's last race of his juvenile season.

Since Man o' War ran his Futurity at Belmont Park after the track surface was intentionally improved for speed, it is not equitable – also stated previously – to compare his time directly with Colin's time because Colin ran at Sheepshead Bay in 1907.

Man o' War's winning time was 71.60 s, and Colin's winning time was 71.20 s. This indicates, naturally, that Colin ran faster than Man o' War despite Belmont Park's improvement because Sheepshead Bay was likely slower than Belmont Park after its 1918 modification, as also previously shown.

However, that does not excuse a student of racing history from attempting to make the comparisons as equitable as possible without slighting either horse.

Therefore, since we have seen that the two samples of data from these time periods differ at least close to the significant level, we must consider how we can adjust the times from one sample so that the difference disappears.

We achieve this time correction by a single, perfectly acceptable, manipulation of the t test. The running times for the Futurity at Sheepshead Bay between 1902 and 1909 were: 74.00, 73.00, 71.80, 71.80, 73.60, 71.20, 71.20 and 71.80 seconds, respectively. Their mean is 72.30 s. The Futurity times at Belmont between 1919 and 1924 (its distance was changed to seven furlongs in 1925 and to other lengths later) were: 71.60, 72.20, 71.40, 71.00, 70.40 and 70.80 seconds. The mean for these races is 71.23 s.

Do the two samples different significantly? Although we have already claimed that they marginally differ, we now present a more detailed analysis.

By differ significantly, statisticians generally mean that there is no more than a five-percent chance of finding a difference between the sample means *as great as or greater than* the one actually found if the two samples represent equal-mean populations.

Statisticians denote this chance level by the lower-case Greek letter alpha, or α. The probability described above is then denoted as $\alpha = 0.05$.

For the current example, running the t test gives the probability level $\alpha = 0.056$. Since this value is just above 0.05, the samples are considered to differ marginally. Note that, for this case, a *one-tailed* t test is used in all pair-wise comparisons by applying a single-factor ANOVA with track differences being the single, variable factor.

We do not know the source of this likely significant difference, and the t test cannot tell us. However, part of it is almost certainly related to the different track surface conditions between the courses. Nothing else is known to be obviously different.

Since there is currently no scientific way in which two or more track surfaces can be measured and compared regarding absolute speed equivalency, this question is essentially moot for present and near-future racing enthusiasts and analysts.

More important now, however, is *by how much* the Sheepshead Bay sample values must be adjusted so that the difference in means will no longer be significant. If we can determine a reasonable amount to subtract from the Sheepshead Bay, Saratoga and pre-treatment Belmont Park running times so that the difference between the sample means is no longer considered significant (i.e., it disappears), then we can at least assume that we are more equitably comparing the two horses for their running ability and not giving one or the other an advantage due to faster running surfaces.

Adjusted t Test Results for Colin

The relatively simple procedure for making this adjustment is now described. It is important that the reader consider this example carefully for future reference.

We use a *one-tailed t test* because we see directly from the set of running times, compared side-by-side, that the post-improvement Belmont times are shorter and will thus have a lower average than the other three track conditions.

When we know the direction of the difference between means as we do here, the *one-tailed test is more appropriate* because it gives the more accurate t estimation.

Furthermore, we see, as is not uncommon, that the variances of the samples appear unequal. An F test will show which sample variances, if any, differ significantly.

Basic Formula for Calculating t Values

The formula for calculating t is: $t = (\bar{x}_1 - \bar{x}_2)/\text{SQRT} [MS_w \cdot ((1/n_1) + (1/n_2))]$, where $\bar{x}_1$ and $\bar{x}_2$ represent the means of any two data samples, SQRT means the square root of the expression within the brackets [ ], MS_w is the mean square deviation within groups calculated by the ANOVA, and $1/n_1$ and $1/n_2$ are the reciprocals of the sample sizes, n_1 and n_2. Seventeen degrees of freedom within groups, df_w, are assigned to MS_w.

When the numerical values of these parameters for Sheepshead Bay and post-improved Belmont, for example, are subjected to the t test in Excel, the t value 1.685, as defined by the above formula, is obtained.

The related significance level of the difference between the means of the two samples is 0.056.

Compensating for Significant Differences

The Sheepshead Bay, Saratoga and pre-improved Belmont Park run times *must be adjusted downward* so they do not differ significantly from the improved Belmont Park run times. The ANOVA t test formula just cited achieves this.

Applying that formula to the *original* data sets relative to the improved Belmont Park run times gives the t values: 1.6799, 4.1297 and 1.8001, respectively. These t values indicate that the corresponding sets of run times differ significantly from improved Belmont Park at α levels 0.056, 0.0004 and 0.045, respectively.

The individual run times within each data sample (each track) must now be lowered so the calculated differences among sample means compensate for these values.

The procedure for doing this is straightforward. The number of within-groups degrees of freedom, df_w, for the ANOVA is 17, where df_w is the total number of run times from all four tracks minus the number of tracks being compared. That number is $(8 + 3 + 4 + 6) - 4$, or 17.

Given the three ANOVA t values above, use Appendix C to locate t for $df_w = 17$ at the 0.10 one-tail significance level. The value is 1.333. It guarantees the correct adjusted difference between sample means when the procedure is completed.

Use this t value in the ANOVA t equation to *adjust the difference between the means* of Sheepshead Bay, Saratoga and Pre-improved Belmont tracks versus the improved Belmont Park. The calculated respective differences for non-significance are: 0.846, 1.108 and 1.012. These values determine how much to subtract from the run times at each track to make them statistically equivalent to the improved Belmont Park track.

To reiterate, this procedure indicates **how much each value (run time) in the original sample must be reduced** so that its mean differs **above** the 0.05 level from a comparison sample's mean. Therefore, 0.224

is subtracted from each Sheepshead Bay data value to *adjust its longer running times downward* and thus more fairly match them against the shorter improved Belmont Park times.

The foregoing procedure is completed for Saratoga and the pre-improved Belmont Park tracks when the respective values 2.332 s and 0.358 s are subtracted from their run times. The resulting re-calculated values then leave the difference between the means of the run times for the three tracks and the mean of the improved Belmont Park track significant above the 0.05 level. This implies that none of the tracks now differ significantly from improved Belmont Park by most statistical criteria.

In other words, due compensation against bias has been achieved.

This obviously takes work. However, most standard statistics texts don't discuss this technique, and it's perfectly legitimate besides being extremely valuable.

Denouement for t

For the present case, the above adjustments and concomitant discussion were essentially academic because Colin's time for the Futurity was already faster than Man o' War's. The obvious conclusion is that now his time will be even faster by comparison. However, there is a bit more to discuss on this topic.

First, however, we show how the effects of changing each of Colin's running times for his juvenile season, for his Saratoga, Sheepshead Bay and pre-improved Belmont track races, change his linear trend results, as they must. Therefore, his predicted running times for the selected comparison distances with Man o' War's are also changed.

Modifications of Colin's Run Times

Recall that Colin raced twelve times during his juvenile season in 1907. Of those twelve races, five were at the pre-improved Belmont Park track, three were at Sheepshead Bay, and two were at Saratoga.

Thus, ten of Colin's twelve races will have modified times. The original times and modified times are given below. For brevity, the abbreviations used are: She = Sheepshead Bay, Sar = Saratoga, Bel = Pre-Belmont and Bri = Brighton Beach. The list is in chronological order, beginning with Colin's maiden race and concluding with his twelfth race of the year. No adjustment is made for Brighton Beach because there is no reasonable way to determine how it would compare with pre- and post-Belmont Park.

Race	Original Time	Adjustment	New Time
Bel, 29May07, 5f	1:01.00	-0.36 s	1:00.64
Bel, 1Jun07, 5f	0:58.00	-0.36s	0:57.64
Bel, 5Jun07, 5.5f	1:06.60	-0.36 s	1:06.24
She, 29Jun07, 6fr	1:12.40	-0.22 s	1:12.18
Bri, 27Jul07, 6f	1:12.20	0.00 s	1:12.20
Sar, 10Aug07, 6f	1:12.00	-2.32 s	1:09.68
Sar, 14Aug07, 6f	1:13.00	-2.32 s	1:10.68
She, 31Aug07, 6f	1:11.20	-0.22 s	1:10.98
She, 7Sep07, 7f	1:24.80	-0.22 s	1:24.58
Bri, 30Sep07, 6f	1:12.60	0.00 s	1:12.60
Bel, 7Oct07, 6f	1:12.00	-0.36 s	1:11.64
Bel, 16Oct07, 7f	1:23.00	-0.36 s	1:22.64

Comparing Linear Estimate Times for Colin and Man o' War

Using the adjusted data just derived for Colin, the following results are obtained. The unadjusted linear estimate times are first given for stated distances followed by the adjusted times.

Colin's Unadjusted Linear Trend

$\hat{y} = 97.00x - 0.68$; COD = 0.9856; standard error = 0.952.
Estimated times for stated distances:
5 f: 59.95 s; 5.5 f: 66.01 s; 6 f: 72.07 s; 7 f: 84.20 s

Colin's Adjusted Linear Trend Using the one-tailed t Test

$\hat{y} = 97.05x - 1.31$; COD = 0.9786; standard error = 1.167

Estimated times for stated distances:
5 f: 59.35 s; 5.5 f: 65.41 s; 6 f: 71.48 s; 7 f: 83.61 s

Man o' War's Unadjusted Linear Trend

$\hat{y} = 95.60x + 0.48$; COD = 0.9723; standard error = 0.901
Estimated times for stated distances:
5 f: 60.24 s; 5.5 f: 66.22 s; 6 f: 72.19 s; 7 f: 84.14 s

As expected, Man o' War's linear trend (not adjusted because he ran on an improved track compared to Colin) yields all times slower than Colin's. His time for seven furlongs needs further explanation.

Comparing Colin and Man o' War: Six Furlongs Only

The linear trends may be slightly biased because both horses did not run the same distances. Since their respective linear trends do not cover exactly the same range of distances, there is more chance for error in approximating how fast either horse would run the set of distances.

Colin, for instance, ran all the stated linear trend distances, but Man o' War did not run a seven-furlong race during his juvenile season. However, both horses did run multiple races at six furlongs, and these common-distances yield the best comparisons.

In analyzing their mutual six-furlong data, we find that Colin ran seven such races. He averaged 72.20 s with a standard deviation of 0.565 s before t-test adjustments and 71.42 s with a standard deviation of 1.036 s after t-test adjustments. His corresponding pre-adjusted and post-adjusted linear trend estimates for this same distance were as given above, 72.07 s and 71.48 s average with standard deviations of 0.95 s and 1.167 s, respectively. The adjusted linear trend results naturally differ from the original data.

Although these values compare favorably, only the data for actual six-furlong races run after t-test adjustments will be used for comparison with Man o' War. The latter's time and standard deviations for the set of six-furlong races are 72.21 s and 0.72 s, respectively. These two horses are thus extremely close, no matter how the statistics are viewed.

One additional comment, however, must be made regarding these races, and then we address the limits analyses of the two horses running at six furlongs.

The Kinetic Energy Formula and Impost Effect

The post-ANOVA t test was used cautiously (above the 0.05 significance level) in attempting to correct for advantages Man o' War might have over Colin, since Man o' War's races at both Belmont Park and Saratoga followed track improvements.

However, one additional datum must be considered so that conditions between the two horses are optimally adjusted. That element is weight carried, or impost. This problem was alluded to in chapter 3 and is now presented in greater detail.

Man o' War's past performance charts show that he carried 130 pounds for five of his six-furlong races. He carried 127 pounds for the sixth of these races. At six furlongs, Colin carried between 122 and 129 pounds, depending on the race.

Can it be accurately determined how impost affected the running times for these colts, assuming that we have already adjusted the track effect equitably via the t test? The answer is yes, and it is more easily done than was the former adjustment.

The standard formula from basic physics for kinetic energy, generally called the energy of motion, is: $KE = \frac{1}{2} \cdot m \cdot v^2$. In this formula, m stands for the mass of an object and v stands for its velocity. For our purposes, we can simply use the weight, w, as a substitute for mass (only the factor 32.2 makes them differ; since that factor remains constant for these calculations, the results remain proportionally equivalent). The average speed of the horses, rather than their velocity, is used. Technically, velocity is not the appropriate entity to use for a running horse because velocity implies a given speed in a specified direction. However, horses are nearly always changing direction during a race, and that dictates using average speed.

How, then, is the formula for KE used to determine how impost affects speed and hence the time for running a race?

First, solve the KE equation in terms of v. This gives: $v = SQRT$

(2KE/w). Then pick some race the horses had in common and calculate the kinetic energies each horse averaged during the race carrying their assigned imposts.

For example, in the Futurity, Colin carried 125 pounds and had an average speed of 55.79 ft/s, since he ran six furlongs (3960 ft) in 70.98 s, after time adjustment by the t test.

Therefore, his KE for that race was ½ · 125 · $(55.79)^2$ = 194,535.29 units. To find what his speed would be if he carryied 127 pounds in the same race, multiply the calculated value of KE by 2 and divide by 127. Then take the square root. The answer is v = 55.35 ft/s. With that new value for speed, divide the race distance, 3960 ft, by 55.35 ft/s. The new time estimate for Colin is then 71.55 s. This implies that the increase of two pounds impost would slow his time from 70.98 s to 71.55 s. This 0.57 s difference, although theoretical, seems reasonable, and it is substantiated by a scientific formula.

Doing the same procedure for Man o' War, his speed is found to increase from 55.31 ft/s when carrying 127 pounds to 55.75 ft/s if he carried only 125 pounds impost. This, in turn, means that his new time would be 71.03 s. This would beat Colin's adjusted time by 0.52 s.

Given the fact that several levels of approximation have been used to reach this point in comparing the two horses, and that the sample size is small, this time is so close that – if it is approximately accurate – the two horses ran virtually equal Futurities.

Linear trends and t adjustments have now been thoroughly examined. It is time to compare these two great champions using the third and final method of this book – Limits Analysis, abbreviated LA.

The Merits and Implications of Limits Analysis

We come now to the final comparison method between Colin's and Man o' War's data for their six-furlong races only. To reiterate, the six-furlong data is the most complete existing, and arguably equivalent, data for either horse. It therefore most fairly estimates their juvenile racing ability. No other choice is available.

Testing Distribution Normalcy

It is first necessary to determine that the time distributions for each horse's six-furlong races each test normal or approximately normal. The Shapiro-Wilk test is used to achieve this. Since Colin ran seven such races and Man o' War ran six, the Shapiro-Wilk test can be used because it requires data samples having three or more values.

Without introducing a lengthy and perhaps confusing explanation, suffice it to say that when the Shapiro-Wilk test is run on the two samples, they both test normal. The tested probability levels for normality are 0.672 and 0.691 for Colin and Man o' War's run time distributions, respectively.

Since each of these values is well above 0.05, we may assume that both samples came from normally distributed populations. This enables us to proceed with limits analysis.

Limits Analysis First Version: NORMDIST

Chapter 1 emphasized that the area under the normal distribution is precisely partitioned between each range of standard deviations. The total area under the normal curve between plus and minus three standard deviations is 99.73 percent.

For all practical purposes, this is considered one hundred percent in terms of estimating the likely number of wins and losses each horse would be assigned by comparing their distributions. And this is what limits analysis involves.

Figure 5 gives a direct comparison between the time distributions at six furlongs for both Colin and Man o' War. The two normal curves in Figure 5 are based on the average and standard deviation values for each horse, after adjustments were made for the heavier imposts Man o' War carried and for the likely slower tracks on which Colin ran – both these factors now having been thoroughly discussed.

When these adjustments were made, Colin's average and standard deviation for his seven six-furlong races were 72.33 s and 0.7859 s. The corresponding values for Man o' War were 72.21 s and 0.6563 s, respectively.

The six-furlong races, considered in isolation, comprise populations. Thus, n was used for calculating the standard deviations, rather than n – 1 as for samples. This is a technical but required nicety which, for this case, does not significantly alter the results.

Entering these values into the Excel spreadsheet in the format appropriate for generating normal curves, results in Figure 5.

Figure 5

Normal Curves: Colin and Man o' War at Six Furlongs

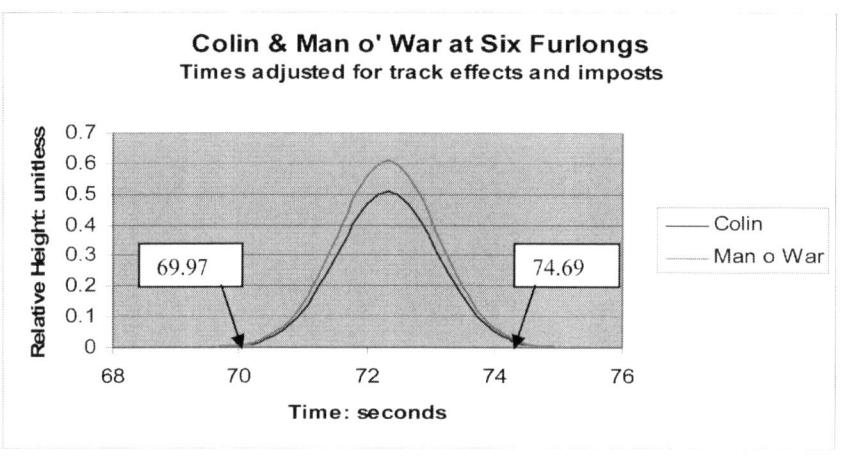

Note that the two points where the curves intersect are labeled with the corresponding value on the time axis. This value is obtained by touching the curve in the Excel spreadsheet with the cursor arrow. These values are required in order to apply the first of two limits analysis techniques that will be used to estimate how many of one hundred 6 f races each horse is likely to win based on the parameters characterizing his normal curve.

The NORMDIST Estimation Method

The first technique involves using the NORMDIST function which comes with Excel's statistical application package. This function allows one to specify any point under a normal curve, for instance the average value, and Excel will calculate the proportion of the area under the curve *to the left of that value*. For the average or mean, Excel gives the value 0.500 since 50 percent of the area under the normal curve is to the left of the mean.

By specifying, in succession, the three areas to the left of 69.97, between 69.97 and 74.69 and above 74.69, as indicated in Figure 5, Excel allows one, by appropriate additions and subtractions, to determine what percent of area in each of the three regions is shared by or controlled separately by both horses.

Knowing these values, one then assigns one win or one loss to *each percentage point of area*, as appropriate for each horse.

For example, when the above procedure is done for the curves in Figure 5, it indicates that Man o' War and Colin would virtually split 50 of 100 matches.

Remember that the adjustments which were made both for possible track effects and impost differences using kinetic energy are not absolute. Some error is probably involved, but that cannot be helped due to the nature of statistics. In this regard, the time values used to generate the two normal curves in Figure 5 may or may not favor one horse over the other. An effort was made to minimize that occurrence, but it would be less than honest not to remind the reader of the possibility.

Having stated these caveats, Colin and Man o' War appear virtually identical in their ability to run six furlongs, based on NORMDIST calculations.

Remember too that the sample sizes, seven for Colin and six for Man o' War, are considered small. This fact also increases the likelihood of error. Insofar as these results go, the 50/50 split does not differ significantly from what one could get on any sequence of tossing a fair coin 100 times and noting the number of heads or tails obtained.

Limits Analysis Second Version: Random Number Generation

Remembering the previous cautions, we now apply the second approach to limits analysis, using Excel's Random Number Generator. This is abbreviated as the RND function in Excel.

This method is much more straightforward to explain, and it is faster to apply. One need not be involved with the manual additions and subtractions of the NORMDIST method of estimation. The RND, however, is a good check of the NORMDIST function.

Basically, to compare the two normal distributions using RND, one simply opens the Excel function from the appropriate menu and fills in the dialog box that appears. That box asks for the mean and standard deviation of the distribution from which one wishes to draw random numbers, plus how many numbers are desired. Again, one hundred random numbers drawn from a normal distribution for each horse are sufficient to judge their relative merits based on their data for running six furlongs.

Using the same means and standard deviations as for the NORMDIST function, five separate 'match races' of one-hundred trials each were run.

The results were, in the order obtained:

Colin:	44	37	39	48	48
Man o' War:	56	63	61	52	52

These results seem to favor Man o' War, given that the parameters of the two normal distributions seem nearly equal. Therefore, five related t tests were performed on random samples of thirty from each of the random number sequences from each above simulation. The t values are: 0.148, 0.176, 0.047, 0.069, and 0.203 for the five sets of simulations. Only one of these values is significant at the 0.05 level. This implies that the mean run times of the five simulations do not differ significantly, despite possible appearances.

This having been clearly stated, the reader must reach his or her own conclusions. The techniques presented in this chapter can then be modified to devise independent studies which may prove more satisfying. Such an exploratory approach is, after all, the interesting and challenging part of applying statistics both creatively and properly.

If nothing else is served by this discussion, it at least permits one to see more clearly just how involved a truly honest and complete analysis of small-sample data is. This makes it all the more apparent that personal opinions about equine greatness, unsubstantiated by any data or analytical method whatsoever, are but empty wind gusts regarding a judgment one way or the other. They are, in this regard, similar to what has been said of the Pentagon – they are like a five-sided wind tunnel.

Take them, therefore, with the proverbial grain of salt.

Casting strife and other related consternation aside, it is time now to speak of two of the truly great fillies ever to run upon this earth – Ruffian and Landaluce.

The following chapters introduce them in the chronological order in which they raced. After their biographies and comparisons are completed, brief statements on five key thoroughbreds – two colts and three fillies – not specifically highlighted in this study will be made, especially regarding why they were excluded. They deserve no less than this considering that their greatness, however measured, is no more in doubt than that the earth, at least somewhere, gets wet when it rains. Their names are: Sysonby, Secretariat, First Flight, La Prevoyante and Personal Ensign.

Ruffian

And when he had opened the third seal, I heard the third beast
say, Come and see. And I beheld, and lo a black horse; and
he that sat on him had a pair of balances in his hand. And I
heard a voice in the midst of the four beasts say, A measure of
wheat for a penny, and three measures of barley for a penny;
and see thou hurt not the oil and the wine." -- Rev. 6:5-6

CHAPTER 5

Ruffian
(1972 – 1975)

Officially, a dark seal brown - but essentially black - filly was foaled at Claiborne Farm near Paris, Kentucky on Monday, April 17, 1972. Her birth was eventually to shake the thoroughbred racing world, but it came exactly two months to the date before another event, the infamous Watergate scandal, would existentially shake American politics and society.

This filly would eventually run even more swiftly than the five Watergate burglars wished they could, and she would certainly become more emblematic of what was good in America than was the highly misguided attempt to smear one political party by another.

It was, in fact, a time of grave overlapping crises within this country. The Vietnam War, though winding down, was still in progress – claiming lives and dividing factions of society as efficiently, if not more so, than any war has ever done.

That conflict would not officially be history until the Paris Peace Accords were signed on Saturday, January 27, 1973, some 285 days after her birth. And still another 559 days would linger dismayingly over this land before Richard Milhous Nixon, 37th President of the United States, would be forced to resign his office.

From the day of that resignation, Ruffian would be allowed less than a year of life – but what a glorious legacy to racing and to the hearts of equine lovers she would leave! Hers would be a gift that all the machinations of the misnamed 'Best and Brightest' within an administration better left for texts on political ethics to ponder, could never tarnish.

Pedigree

But her ability on the track should scarcely have been a surprise, so overflowing was her genetic cup with the special wine known as thoroughbred blood.

One need regress but a single generation in her pedigree, and all that needs articulation cries loudly to the attentive.

Her sire was Reviewer, and her grandsire on the tail-male side was none other than Bold Ruler. Aside from generally being considered the greatest all-time American sire of champion thoroughbreds, one of his sons, the eventually immortal Secretariat, was already poised on stage that April day to fashion a juvenile year over which journalists would gush superlatives that were effete and jejune understatements, so beautifully and elegantly did he run.

But this was just the start. For Ruffian's dam, Shenanigans, was sired by the undisputedly great Native Dancer. He would eventually race twenty-two times between 1952 and 1954. He would win twenty-one of those races, twice by as much as nine lengths, and lose just once – and that by a head - in the Kentucky Derby to Dark Star.

As some horses' only claims to fame were that they had once bested Kelso, so Dark Star's was undoubtedly that he was the only horse to beat Native Dancer.

In all, Ruffian's immediate pedigree within the first three generations preceding her Sire and Dam contain three horses, Polynesian, Discovery (once on each side of her pedigree) and Challedon, all of whom are listed in the top 487 champions of the twentieth century by Daily Racing Form (3).

Those Helping Shape her Destiny

Additional facts are that her breeders and owners were the same, Stuart and Barbara Janney, owners of Locust Hill Farm in Glyndon, Maryland, that her trainer was Frank Y. Whiteley Jr. and that her jockey, for all but two of her eleven career races, was Jacinto Vasquez. Vince Bracciale Jr. rode her for those two efforts.

As of 2003, Frank Y. Whiteley Jr. was listed as tied with Bob Wheeler in the number thirty-one position on the all-time list of trainers' victories in major North American Races. (10).

In that same year, Jacinto Vasquez ranked number fourteen among jockeys for in-the-money finishes in major North American Races, and Vince Bracciale Jr. ranked one-hundred twenty-two.

Physical Impression

Ruffian was physically imposing. She was considered large for a filly – nearly seventeen hands; her girth was also exceptional. One might call her temperament "keen," for lack of a better descriptor. She was, as aptly stated by author Jane Schwartz, 'burning from the start' (11).

Summary: Her Juvenile Season

Ruffian's juvenile season lasted from Wednesday, May 22, 1974 until Friday, August 23, 1974. It began at Belmont Park and ended at Saratoga.

She ran five times. Her first three races were at five and one-half furlongs; her last two races were at six furlongs. Jacinto Vasquez rode her three times, and Vince Bracciale Jr. rode her twice during this season.

The essence of those five races follows. Hers is a story of brilliance from the beginning until the end. Probably only one other American filly, Landaluce, was her equal as a two-year-old.

The next chapter belongs to Landaluce, and the chapter after that provides a comparison between these two remarkable fillies with no attempt to judge them one way or the other. The reader is left to his or her own predilections regarding judgment.

Maiden Voyage – a Special Weights Event

On Wednesday, May 22, 1974, the filly Ruffian, essentially unknown to the racing public, was guided into gate number nine for the day's third race at Belmont Park. It was set for a five and a half-furlong run and was classed as a 'Maiden Special Weights' race. The track was rated fast, and her rider was Jacinto Vasquez. She carried 116 pounds.

Eight of the ten entrants had already taken their gate positions by the time Ruffian was settled in, and only one other, to her right on the outside, remained to be positioned.

When the gates finally opened wide with their customary clang, the spectators saw a remarkable thing, remarkable at least in the world of thoroughbred racing. They watched fairly stunned as that rare event, the thoroughbred destined to win multiple stakes races without losing, exited gate nine, slowly at first but then fast becoming an inky black blur which left the other horses plodding in its wake.

With mane and tail alternately furling and unfurling, alone in her own slipstream, Ruffian proceeded past the quarter-, half-, and five-eighths mile calls in times of 22.20, 45.00 and 57.00 seconds.

She led by three lengths at the quarter mile, by five at the half mile and by eight at the five-eighths-mile call. When she crossed the finish, the nearest competitor of the other nine horses was Suzest. Suzest was fifteen lengths back, and this was just a five and one- half-furlong sprint.

A mere 63.00 total seconds had elapsed since the gates opened, and the legend of Ruffian began to grow from that nearly literal minute onward. Could she but speak, she might have correctly told Whiteley on leaving the paddock, "See you in a minute, Frank."

Just incidentally, Ruffian equaled the track record with her run. But was this perhaps simply good fortune? Was this first day of her racing life just when she happened to peak? Mr. Whiteley is said to have wondered this aloud. The answer was not long in coming.

The Fashion Stakes

Three weeks passed. It was now Wednesday, June 12, and the race was the eighth of the day at Belmont Park. Again Vasquez rode her, but another pound of impost had been added, making her burden 117 pounds. Despite this addition, her trainer, Frank Whiteley, felt she was well prepared and looking fit.

This was the Fashion Stakes, an event rated G-3. It was another five and one half-furlong outing for Ruffian, and the Belmont surface was again rated fast. Her competition had already dropped to five. News of racing excellence travels quickly.

Ruffian resumed where she left off three weeks earlier, much to the crowd's delight. The quarter-mile call was left behind in 22.40 s. She led by one and one-half lengths. Then came the half-mile. She reached that in 45.20 s – still leading by one and one-half lengths.

At the five-eighths point, she had increased her lead to four lengths, the time of 57.00 s exactly matching her pace at that distance in her maiden outing. Apparently the added one pound on her shoulders didn't matter much.

She crossed the finish in 63.00 s flat, duplicating the exact time of her maiden run and leading the second-place filly, Copernica, by six-and-three-quarters lengths.

Ruffian had, for the second consecutive race, equaled the Belmont track record and had set a new Fashion Stakes record. Her trainer was pleased, stating, to the effect, that he hadn't yet set her down – meaning he didn't know just how fast she could go. (12)

The Astoria Stakes

A generous twenty-eight days passed before Ruffian was asked to run again. This time she would try another rider, Vince Bracciale Jr. Jacinto Vasquez and been suspended for ten days for rough riding, but Bracciale was a promising young jockey.

Ruffian would also try carrying another extra pound of impost because she was – well, just making the other thoroughbreds look a bit shabby.

And so, bearing 118 pounds of Mr. Bracciale and tack, Ruffian slipped into gate number two for what would be her last five and one-half furlong race.

One filly was on her left at the rail, and two were outside. Apparently only the trainers and owners of these three fillies thought they had a chance to win.

The Aqueduct surface at Jamaica, New York was fast that day for the Astoria Stakes, another G-3 rated event.

Ruffian, hardly a surprise by now, turned up her speed a notch, perhaps compensating for what she felt was the added weight on her shoulders.

Swiftly the call points flew by – faster, in fact than for her first two events. There were now quarter-miles, half-miles and five-eighths miles of 21.80, 44.40 and 56.40 seconds clocked as Ruffian ran unconcernedly ahead by leads of one, three and six lengths at those respective distances.

At the finish, her closest rival was Laughing Bridge, but she and not her owner or trainer was probably the only one laughing that day. Ruffian decisively beat her by nine lengths. She had now won her first three races by a combined margin of thirty and three-quarters lengths, more than a ten-length average margin of victory.

As fast as she was this day, Ruffian was still one-fifth second slower than the track record. It was, nevertheless, a remarkable run and was a new stakes record.

In all fairness, it must be noted that the track variant that day was a plodding 15. This indicates that the average race of the same length on the same track for that day was run three seconds slower (15/5 s) than the track record.

While this number undoubtedly indicates some combination of slowness due to both track condition and horses' ability, it at least gives reason to suspect that the track was partially to blame for the slower times.

Ruffian was undoubtedly reassuring everyone of her ability. She had carried successively heavier imposts in each of her races, and she kept burning up the tracks. It appeared that the sky was the limit for this spirited, ebony-coated filly.

The Sorority Stakes

The scene now shifted to Monmouth Park, New Jersey. It was Saturday, July 27, 1974 and time for the Sorority Stakes, Ruffian's first G-1 stakes effort. A crowd of about 26,000 awaited the start. Jacinto Vasquez was up again, and so would be Ruffian's impost – to 119 pounds. In horseracing, both time and weight march on.

She now faced only three other fillies, but this would be her first six-furlong test. The track was rated fast, and Ruffian drew post position number three.

Although the field was small, one of those fillies was supposedly a real speedster, with the appropriate name 'Hot n Nasty.'

Ruffian, however, didn't seem to mind the extra half furlong at all and apparently was unconcerned about both Hot n Nasty's reputation and the extra poundage. Her final time of 69.00 s was just 6.20 s longer than for her previous race, which was one-half furlong, or one-sixteenth of a mile, less.

Although she won by two and one-quarter lengths over Hot n Nasty, she did not break or tie the track record. The Daily Racing Form charts show her speed rating/track variant as 95-15 for the Sorority Stakes. This means that she was one full second slower (five-fifths second) than the track record while the average of the day's races was three seconds slower than the record. However, she had again set a new stakes record.

Recall that the second number of that compound statistic, the '15,' indicates that the average time for races the same length and on the same surface for that day were a full three seconds slower (15/5 seconds) than the record of the past three years. So, in fact, Ruffian was a full two seconds faster than the average time for six-furlong races on that day – which means she was also faster than most of the colts.

The Spinaway Stakes

The summer of 1974 was about two-thirds past now. Friday, August 23 arrived and, with it, the time for the eighty-fourth running of the Spinaway Stakes, Ruffian's second G-1 stakes effort and the final race of her juvenile year.

Vince Bracciale Jr. was aboard once more, Mr. Vasquez again being penalized by the stewards as a naughty boy, this time for seven days. Ruffian's impost was, unsurprisingly, up. Now she would carry 120 pounds. Would this burden finally even the odds for her foes?

Any hope to that effect was brief, for there would be no such luck for her competition, despite the best machinations of the racing stewards.

For the second and final time or her juvenile season, Vince Bracciale Jr. settled himself on her back, adjusting his feet in the irons and firming his grip on the reins. Perhaps it was somewhat lucky for Ruffian that he was riding.

She was, for the second time that year, assigned post position number two. That was as close to the rail that she ever started that year, and Vince Bracciale Jr. was aboard both times.

The big black-brown filly didn't disappoint the crowd. Perhaps she wished to show the stewards once again that weight didn't matter at all.

Out the clanging number-two slot she went, breaking second in the four-horse field and proceeding to click off times of 22.20 s and 44.80 s at the quarter- and half-mile calls. Her final time of 68.60 s saw her finish a comfortable twelve and three-quarter lengths ahead of Laughing Bridge – that filly's second defeat in both attempts to test Ruffian.

Her time set a Spinaway Stakes record and just missed the track record by three-fifths of a second.

Ruffian's time was, in fact, the fastest for six furlongs by a juvenile of either sex at Saratoga. It was also the second-fastest time of the entire 1974 Saratoga season. For the remaining nineteen years that the Spinaway remained a six-furlong race at Saratoga, no filly ever ran a faster time than Ruffian. Even Canada's outstanding La Prevoyante took 70.80 s in her three-length Spinaway victory.

It was an exhilarating way to cap Ruffian's juvenile season. For these five splendid efforts, Ruffian was named U.S. Champion 2yo Filly of 1974.

Praise from a Master

One can heap many facts and superlatives each upon the other, *ad infinitum et ad nauseam*, and still not capture an iota of Ruffian's essence. She was unique.

Perhaps the solitary and most meaningful praise of all came from a modest and self-effacing Canadian gentleman named Lucien Lauren, Secretariat's trainer.

His praise carries special weight. He has been quoted as saying, sometime after the Spinaway Stakes, "As God is my judge, she might be better than Secretariat." (12).

Ironically, it may be the related attempt to prove Ruffian better than most good colts that cost her life.

She was entered in a match race against Foolish Pleasure, winner of the 1975 Kentucky Derby, in what was to be the final race of her sophomore year and probably of her career. Foolish Pleasure was an excellent colt that barely missed a Triple Crown that year in losing by a length in the Preakness and by a nose in the Belmont.

Ruffian was leading Foolish Pleasure by about three-quarters of a length at near the three-quarter pole of the ten-furlong run when her right front ankle snapped.

The rest is one of the most tragic tales of thoroughbred racing history. The great Ruffian never recovered. She made it through surgery but thrashed about so much after the sedation wore off that she had to be euthanized. She was interred in the infield of Belmont Park with her head facing the finish line. It is said that the noted sports writer and Secretariat's distinguished biographer, William Nack, essentially quit covering thoroughbred racing shortly after Ruffian's death. But if Ruffian was comparable to Secretariat, so, of necessity, was Landaluce – the filly described in the following chapter.

Landaluce

*And when he had opened the fourth seal, I heard the voice of
the fourth beast say, Come and see. And I looked, and behold a
pale horse: and his name that sat on him was Death, and Hell
followed with him. And power was given unto them over the
fourth part of the earth, to kill with sword, and with hunger, and
with death, and with the beasts of the earth. -- Rev. 6:7-8*

CHAPTER 6

Landaluce

(1980 – 1982)

Introduction

It seemed as though something unsavory was always brewing in
American politics, and the year of Landaluce's birth proved no exception.
On Saturday, February 2 of 1980, an FBI investigation, code name Abscam,
of undercover bribery allegations ended by implicating one U.S. senator,
seven House members and thirty-one sundry government officials.

It was beginning to seem that horses were the only denizens of
America not directly concerned with unethical behavior.

Fortunately for American morale, but in a totally different environ-
ment, a dark bay brown filly, with a pedigree to choke a horse – pun partially intended – entered life at Spendthrift Farm in the Commonwealth
of Kentucky. Her owners named her for a Spanish ranch guide, Francisco
Landaluce (pronounced: Lan-da-LU-cy).

The great Seattle Slew was her sire, and a racy little number – yes, too
many puns in quick succession – called Strip Poker was her dam. Seattle
Slew, it so happened, was ranked the ninth best thoroughbred racehorse
of the 20th Century by the Blood-Horse, Inc. in 1999. (2).

He is noted in that publication as the only horse that will enter the 21st Century to win a Triple Crown while undefeated. 'Slew', as he came to be affectionately called, raced three years, at ages two through four. He had seventeen starts. Of those efforts, he won fourteen times, nine of which were stakes races. He placed twice, both in stakes races. He finished out of the money just once. That was on Sunday, July 3, 1977 at Hollywood Park in the Swaps G-1 Stakes race when he finished fourth.

Her story gets better, however. Landaluce's paternal grandsire was Bold Reasoning whose sire was Boldnesian whose sire was Bold Ruler. And so she came packaged with some of the same blood that surged through Secretariat. On her dam's side there was maternal grandsire Bold Bidder whose sire was Bold Ruler whose sire was Nasrullah. She therefore carried a double genetic dose of Secretariat.

Thus, reversing time just four generations for the filly Landaluce yields a genetic stew of contributions from no less than five major champion thoroughbreds, since it may now be added that Hail to Reason, Round Table and Myrtle Charm were also her direct ancestors.

This admixture of genes turned out tremendously efficacious for owners L. R. French and Barry Beal, trainer D. Wayne Lukas and jockey Laffit Pincay Jr. who rode Landaluce in all of her juvenile, and only, races.

In five races, beginning on Saturday, July 3, 1982 and ending on Saturday, October 23 of that year, Landaluce won five straight times by a combined winning margin of forty-six and one-half lengths – an average win margin of 9.3 lengths.

She was awarded – posthumously, for she died on Saturday, December 11 from an intestinal infection – the title American Champion 2yo Filly for 1982. There could have been no other choice. Let us review her amazing story now.

Maiden Special Weights Race – Hollywood Park

On Saturday, July 3, 1982, Landaluce departed gate number six at

Hollywood Park in a six-furlong sprint featuring seven entrants. She laid back in number two position for a while but was leading by one and one-half lengths at call point one, the quarter mile.

She then just seemed to draw gracefully and assuredly away – Pincay's bright emerald green silks with white polka dots flapping in the breeze for the other jockey's to enjoy.

By the finish, which occurred just 68.20 seconds after her gate departure, Landaluce had 'broken her maiden' by seven lengths. She caused quite a stir for the almost casual manner in which she seemed to run.

The decision was made to run her a second time just a week later in the Hollywood Lassie Stakes, a G-2 level event.

Another Six Furlongs at Hollywood Park

As far as pure talent, as evidenced by a breathtaking acceleration, the Hollywood Lassie Stakes of Saturday, July 10, 1982 was undoubtedly Landaluce's pièce de résistance.

She appeared to be battling with the then undefeated Barzell until near the stretch. Just to make sure that she was paying attention to running, Pincay chirped and tapped her on the shoulder and she simply exploded, so it seemed, like some exotic racing machine going through higher and higher gears.

She finished in the time of 68.00 seconds flat for the six furlongs, still said to be the fastest clocking ever for a juvenile filly in a one-turn race of that distance.

Pincay himself said he had never expected her to take off that suddenly, adding that he had never been on a horse so young that could accelerate so smoothly and quickly. In fact, her fractions at the half-mile and five-eights-mile calls plus her final time indicate that she accelerated throughout the race's entire final quarter mile.

She gained twelve of the entire 21 lengths of her winning margin over Bold Out Line, with Barzell finishing third, between the half-mile pole and the finish line.

And yet she gave the impression she was relaxed – simply galloping, her ears pricked, and apparently giving little real effort.

The Third Outing: Del Mar Debutante Stakes

A long rest ensued for Landaluce. She would not run again until Sunday, September 5. That was at Del Mar Racetrack in the eighth race of the day, the Del Mar Debutante G-2 Stakes event.

This would be a one-mile run, her longest effort thus far. Her weight assignment was 119 pounds, up two pounds from the 117 she carried in her first two races.

Landaluce left her gate, number four, again in rather leisurely fashion. She was totally unlike Ruffian in this regard. Ruffian seemed to abhor having horses ahead of her, for Ruffian led at every call point in every race she ran, amazing as that may sound.

But Landaluce apparently preferred to pace herself a bit, or perhaps she was simply toying with her rivals. We will never know. Some creatures, the very intelligent ones, do play games similar to those of humans. Anyone who observes animals intently can tell you that – but consider the following digression.

Digression: The Blue Jay, the Tabby and Animal Mentality

Once, for instance, I watched a Blue Jay in the neighbor's front yard, searching for food on the ground. The neighbor's yellow tabby suddenly appeared from around the corner of the house and started stalking toward the bird.

My first thought was that, unless I intervened, the bird was as good as cooked.

But as I started to rise from my chair and the cat was within some six or seven feet of his feathered prey, the Jay hopped about two feet up onto the nearby branch of a dogwood tree.

This surprised me, and I relaxed. I sat down again but continued watching.

Stealthily, the cat began climbing the tree and finally reached the branch where the Blue Jay had alighted. As the tabby began crawling out on the branch, the Jay hopped up another couple feet to another branch – just beyond reach.

The cat turned, reached the tree's trunk again and climbed up to the next level. This scene repeated at least four or five times until the Jay was at the topmost point of the tree, some twenty feet above earth. Still the cat apparently suspected nothing.

By that time the branches were too weak to properly support him, and the tabby bobbed up and down in mid-air, looking quite puzzled regarding what had happened.

The Jay then merely flew away, undoubtedly voicing the avian equivalent of scornful laughter at the stupidity of warm-blooded mammals. So much for evolution!

So, who knows what Landaluce was thinking? Perhaps about her next race and what fun it would be dusting all those poor unsuspecting fillies.

Returning now to the Del Mar Debutante – Landaluce bore her 119 pound impost proudly. It didn't seem to affect her. She trailed by a half length at the quarter-mile call; then she led by increments of a head at the half mile, by one and one-half lengths at three-quarters of a mile and by six and one-half lengths at the finish.

Her time was 95.60 seconds for the mile, or 1:35.60 in standard racing notation.

More than a month would now pass before her next effort.

First Time at Santa Anita

The Anoakia Stakes were scheduled for running at Santa Anita Racetrack on Monday, October 11, 1982. It was a G-3 level race, and it would be the last time Landaluce would run at that low a level.

As always, her jockey would be Pincay. The distance was seven furlongs, considered the longest of the sprint distances. There were eight total entrants, an appropriate number for those devotees of numerology, since the race would be the eighth of the day. To make things even more "fateful" for those placing stock in such happenings, Landaluce drew gate position number eight.

All this turned out to be the verified superstition that it is. When she and her 123 pounds (which only add to 6!) of jockey and tack, the heaviest burden she would shoulder in her brief career, left the gate, she was in second place. As was typical, she nearly looked as though she was loitering, deciding whether or not she really wished to bother running past all these horses.

As it was true that Ruffian was never headed at a call point, Landaluce was rarely ahead, especially in the early going of a race. That simply seemed to be her style.

In fact, at the first call, the quarter-mile, she was in third by a neck. But then she began running. She led by two lengths at the half mile, by a generous eight lengths at the three-quarter mile and won easily by ten lengths over Rare Thrill in a time of 1:21.80 s. Time of Sale was third, another one and one-quarter lengths in arrears.

To all observing this run, it was simply business as usual as far as the lovely dark brown filly was concerned.

Now, as it sadly turned out, Landaluce had but two more races to run. She would win the first, but she would suffer her only defeat in the second. That would be the meeting with the etiologically uncertain Colitis X -- for her, the apocalyptic Pale Horse.

The Hands of Time

There are, it seems, some events, people and creatures that one wishes never to end or to leave us. A lovely refrain from Michel LeGrand's music (13) elegantly captures what we often wish could be done to prolong the highest goods we experience in life. However, time actually has no hands that we might hold in ours to stop or delay its inexorable passing.

But time, the very existence of which is open to debate among co-gnoscenti, is indifferent, so it seems, to our hands. Thus, twelve days elapsed and Landaluce once again found herself in a starting gate, this time holding position six in a field featuring seven fillies. If the mechanical contrivance that is called a starting gate bothered her at all, she would never need worry about it again.

Santa Anita Redux

It was Saturday, October 23 and it was the second time around for Santa Anita. This final race of her career and too brief sojourn on earth would be her longest – an eight and one-half-furlongs run on a fast track.

It was the Oak Leaf Stakes, her highest graded event, level G-1, entered in five starts. She was assigned 117 pounds, a reversion, so it seemed, to the lightest imposts she carried in her first two juvenile races.

Once more she was rather slow exiting the gate, being third of the seven finely tuned runners.

However, she again found that silky smooth and seemingly effortless stride within a fraction of the first furlong, and she led at the quarter-mile call by a head. Her time was barely on the slow side for her - :22.60 seconds.

But then the calls began flying by faster and faster. She led by three lengths at the half mile, by four lengths at the three-quarter mile and at the wire she was two lengths the winner, pretty much having been put on cruise control by Pincay, over Sophisticated Girl.

Her final time was 1:41.80. She had run and won five times; she was now famous.

Requiem for a Champion

Her owners and her trainer, D. Wayne Lukas, now pointed her for the Grade 1 Hollywood Starlet Stakes. That event was set for Sunday, November 28. By November 22, however, Landaluce was ill. It was at first thought to be nothing alarming – merely a simple virus.

However, it was Colitis X, and it so happened that her immune system was unable to thwart it.

Future plans for running were quickly forgotten as everyone con cerned with her welfare simply began doing all they could to keep her alive.

For whatever ultimate reason, her recovery would not occur. It is tempting to become flowery in expressing possible causes for her death, but death is never really pretty or glorious, no matter the level of prose attending it or attempting to transform it.

However, for those who measure a man neither by his prestige, nor his wealth, nor his number of influential friends but by a totally different standard transcending basic societal norms, then D. Wayne Lukas stands extremely tall by that measure.

On Saturday, December 11, 1982, the lovely and superlative filly named for a Spanish ranch guide died with her head in her trainer's arms.

Unless one has cradled a dying loved one or pet, one has no comprehension of the thoughts and feelings that envelop the mind at that instant when we realize we will never again share our life with them – that something about the world and life has irrevocably changed and that nothing will ever again be as bright.

Some people, in fact, are possessed by terror in anticipating such times and actively flee them. It is to no avail. Those they love die anyway. The Pale Horse never loses.

D. Wayne Lukas did not flee. He stayed until the last breath left her body. He epitomizes, to my thinking, the essence of nobility for that moment, regardless of anything else he has accomplished in his famed career.

Those who loved her buried her by the waterfall in the infield at Hollywood Park, the place where she made her first racing impression, one that lived up to and transcended all conceivable human expectations - a truly remarkable gift from the equine gods.

Later, others who also loved her but were less privileged for first-hand contact did the best they could. They posthumously voted her American Champion 2yo Filly for 1982. It is an honor to be sure, but it is doubtful any human accolade does true homage to a breathtaking talent such as hers.

Jerry Izenberg of Newark's The Star-Ledger once commented to the effect that many people thought Secretariat's Belmont was just another horse race. However, he disagreed because he considered Secretariat an athlete. (14)

Landaluce justly deserves the same accolade.

If it is true that Allah created the horse by summoning the South Wind to condense itself, He surely commanded it twice as emphatically for Landaluce.

There is no such person as a philosopher; no one is detached; the observer, like the observed, is in chains.
-- E. M. Forster

CHAPTER 7

Ruffian and Landaluce: Combined Performance Review

This chapter presents an overview, similar to that of chapter 4, of some statistical techniques which might profitably be used to compare the past performance records of thoroughbred horses such as Ruffian and Landaluce.

It is hereby emphatically re-stated, however, that the following data comparisons are for no purpose other than illustrating the pitfalls that will be encountered, especially with the generally small samples indigenous to thoroughbred racing records.

By no means am I comparing these, by definition, incomparable champions to determine which ran better. Statistics, properly applied and interpreted, cannot reach that conclusion. That being clearly stated, the following descriptions are of essentially the same statistical methods that were used to perform nearly identical informal comparisons of Colin to Man o' War.

Performance Ranking Indicators

The same set of thirteen parameters used to rate Colin and Man o' War contain certain facts which may vary in interpretation, depending upon the researcher.

In this case, no corrections are made for either horse because no exact known differences between running conditions existed for Ruffian and Landaluce as they did for Colin and Man o' War. Both fillies, in other words, represented the same so-called era.

Both Ruffian and Landaluce each ran five races in their juvenile years of 1974 and 1982, respectively. Landaluce ran a wider range of distances, from six furlongs to eight and one-half furlongs, than did Ruffian. Ruffian ran at just two distances – five and one-half and six furlongs. That is the only realistically meaningful difference between their juvenile racing records.

Both of their performance samples are, as has been repeatedly emphasized herein, considered small for statistical analysis purposes. Any statistical sample less then thirty is considered small.

As such, these samples can invite premature conclusions which are subject to gross inaccuracy if proper caution is not taken.

The diligent reader should always consider the caveat: one **never uses statistics to prove** that one horse is better or greater than another. Even with large sample sizes, those equal to or larger than thirty, one cannot justly make such sweeping statements.

The following results of the thirteen comparison categories, however, should at least prove interesting – if not being absolute indicators of equine racing greatness.

The Selected Comparison Factors

The following list of factors (in bold font) gives a comprehensive overview of Ruffian's and Landaluce's juvenile running performances. A brief explanation accompanies some of these numbers, for those cases where the meaning of the factor itself may not be obvious. This intentionally duplicates the format used in chapter 4.

Overall Career Racing Records for Juvenile Year

Ruffian: 5: 5-0-0
Landaluce: 5: 5-0-0

Fastest Average Speed in a Race

Ruffian: 57.80 ft/s. 7/10/1974; 5.5f; fast track; 118 lb. impost
Landaluce: 58.24 ft/s, 7/10/1982; 6f; fast track; 117 lb. impost

Highest Momentum (impost x speed) Generated

Ruffian: 6927 units, 8/23/1974, 6f, fast track, 120 lb. impost
Landaluce: 6947 units, 10/11/1982, 7f, fast track, 123 lb. impost

Explanation: Momentum and kinetic energy are more inclusive indicators of performance than is speed alone. Momentum is more easily calculated. Simply multiply the horse's average speed for a race in feet per second by the impost in pounds. The result indicates an energy of motion that the horse sustained – the actual units being in *pound-feet per second*, but simply called *units* herein since only the numerical value is important. Kinetic energy may also be used for this indicator. It is slightly more awkward to calculate and yields no greater information – still being the energy of motion generated by the horse throughout a given race.

Greatest Action (momentum x distance) Generated

Ruffian: 5195 units, 8/23/1974, 6f, fast track, 120 lb. impost
Landaluce: 6851 units, 10/23/1982, 8.5f, fast track, 117 lb. impost

Explanation: When momentum, as defined above, is multiplied by the distance (in miles) of an entire race, it gives a slightly better perspective or different feeling for how given horses sustained their energy of motion throughout the race. This number naturally varies for different distances and for different imposts depending on the horse. Its units, fully expressed, are *pound-feet squared per second*, since the distance unit is multiplied by the pound-feet per second unit of momentum. Again, merely stating *units* is sufficient for this type of data.

Average Weight Carried (impost) for All Races

Ruffian: 118.00 lbs.
Landaluce: 118.60 lbs.

Average Momentum for All Races

Ruffian: 6801 units
Landaluce: 6715 units

Average Action for All Races

Ruffian: 4847 units
Landaluce: 5941 units

Average Winning Margin (lengths) for All Races

Ruffian: 9.15
Landaluce: 9.30

Most Races Run at a Common Distance

Ruffian: 3 (of 5) at 5.5f
Landaluce: 2 (of 5) at 6f

Average Size of Field per Race

Ruffian: 5.6
Landaluce: 6.6

Average Post Position

Ruffian: 3.8
Landaluce: 5.4

Average Performance Figure

Ruffian: 11.60
Landaluce: 5.80

Explanation: For this study, the Performance Figure was defined as how many fifths of a second the given horse's **Speed Rating** for each race was either better or worse than the average **Track Variant** for all races at the same distance on that day for that track.

For example: suppose a given horse achieved a Speed Rating of 87 for a given race (meaning that his time was 13 fifths of a second (2.6 s) slower than the track record *for the previous three years*, where 100 is defined as the track record) and the Track Variant (how many fifths of a second slower than the track record the *average of all races run that day* was) was 17, or 3.4 s. Therefore, the given horse's Performance Figure in *that race* was four fifths of a second (0.8 s) *better than the average* at *that track* for all races run at *that distance* (100 – 87 = 13; 100 – 83 = 17). Thus, the horse's Performance Figure was 87 – 83 = 4, or 17 – 13 = 4.

The preceding Performance Figures indicate that Ruffian averaged 11.60 fifths of a second (2.32 s) faster than the average winning horse for all her races, and that Landaluce averaged 5.80 fifths of a second (1.16 s) faster than average winning horse for all her races.

Recall that one-fifth of a second is 0.20 s.

Average Track Record Comparison Number

Ruffian: -1.80
Landaluce: -6.80

Explanation: This number was chosen simply to represent how many fifths of a second, on average, the horses *either broke or missed* the track record for all their races. From the above, Ruffian averaged nearly two-fifths of a second (0.40 s) *slower* per race than the existing track record, and Landaluce averaged nearly seven-fifths of a second (1.40 s) *slower* than the existing track record per race. In other words, this gives Ruffian an average Speed Rating of 100 – 1.80 = 98.20 and Landaluce an average Speed Rating of 100 – 6.80 = 93.20, if Speed Ratings were actually expressed in decimal format.

If one wishes to compare the two horses by using the categories above, assign one point for the better score and zero points for the lower score in twelve of the thirteen categories (number of common-distance races not counted). Then Ruffian's point total is 3 and Landaluce's is 8. Such 'facile' ratings should be used cautiously!

Linear Trend Analysis Results

The linear trends for Ruffian and Landaluce are now discussed regarding how each horse is theoretically predicted to run various average distances. Recall that Ruffian ran only two distances during her juvenile year, five and one-half furlongs and six furlongs. Landaluce's races ranged from six furlongs up to and including eight and a-half furlongs. Therefore, projecting times for Ruffian into distances she did not actually run would be subject to greater prediction error, even though her coefficient of determination is nearly as high as Landaluce's and her standard error of the mean is smaller. This is partly a matter of judgment, but the caution is good to heed.

Ruffian and Landaluce: Linear Trends for all Juvenile Races

As was the case for Colin and Man o' War, the basics of computing and interpreting linear trends were described in chapter 1; thus, the results are all that are presented now. All values are rounded to two decimal places, except for the coefficient of determination, R^2, taken to four decimal places to make its percent equivalent obvious.

Ruffian: $\hat{y} = 93.87x - 1.60$; $R^2 = 0.9974$, standard error = 0.19.

Landaluce: $\hat{y} = 108.55 - 13.26$; $R^2 = 0.9998$, standard error = 0.26

When these linear trend equations are used to predict times for the standard distances that either Ruffian or Landaluce would likely run, the following results are obtained, with distances in fractional miles and running times in seconds:

Ruffian:	Miles:	0.6875,	0.75,	0.875,	1.0625
	Times:	62.93,	68.80,	80.53,	98.13
Landaluce:	Miles:	0.6875,	0.75,	0.875,	1.0625
	Times:	61.37,	68.15,	81.72,	102.08

The above data indicate that, using best-predicted linear-trend values, Landaluce was slightly faster than Ruffian at the first two of the four comparison distances, whereas Ruffian is projected to be faster over the latter two distances.

Recall, however, that Ruffian's linear trend analysis is based on only two distances whereas Landaluce's is based on four. This makes it somewhat problematic to insure that Ruffian's linear trend results, especially for longer distances, are unbiased.

Further Considerations

We cannot truly determine whether track conditions affected one horse more than the other as we did for Colin and Man o' War. In the former case we have historical data stating that both Belmont Park and Saratoga were improved for speed only months before Man o' War ran on them.

We can consider, however, whether the different imposts the horses carried, plus several other factors, test significantly different. Ruffian began racing in her maiden carrying 116 pounds. However, she added one pound for each race she entered thereafter, and her final impost was 120 pounds.

Landaluce's imposts were generally more constant. She carried 117 pounds in three of her five races. However, in one race she carried 123 pounds. That was three pounds more than Ruffian carried under her greatest impost.

When a t test is run between the two sets of five imposts each, no significant difference is found. The t value for the comparison is 0.337. This is not considered remotely indicative, i.e., 0.05 or less, that one should suspect one set of imposts differed appreciably from the other. Therefore, we cannot logically say that the impost distributions in their respective five races favored either horse.

Carrying the t test further, we can profitably look at number of starters, post position and Track Variant. Any of these variables certainly can be suspected of having some influence on race outcome. A one-tailed test with unequal variance was used.

None of these factors, however, tests significant between Ruffian and Landaluce. The t test value for number of starters, compared over all five races, is 0.227. The t test value for Post Position held by each horse over five races is 0.171.

Therefore, we cannot say that either horse was favored by impost, number of starters or the respective post positions assigned.

Last, when the Track Variant for each horse over all five races is compared, it also tests non-significant. Recall that the Track Variant is presumed to indicate some combination of track surface effect and quality of the runners. Unfortunately, one cannot separate these two components and determine which is due to track conditions alone.

All we can note is that the respective tracks were rated fast for both horses for each of the five races they ran in their juvenile seasons. The final t test value for Track Variant significance was 0.317. Although this value is considered not significant, what is fast for one track surely does not equate exactly to the speed estimate for a second track.

Both Landaluce and Ruffian had identical average values (2.6) for the grade levels of their races; we thus must assume they faced basically equal quality opponents. However, this certainly is not a scientific measure. A t-test value of 0.500 between their grade levels in general corroborates the preceding conclusion, however.

If the opponents they faced in the course of five races were exactly matched in quality, and *if* they were performing equally during those respective races, then we could state that the above Track Variant effect was due to track conditions alone.

That still changes little, but it clarifies what we face regarding data decisions. In this case the added fact of statistical opponent equality would mean that the differences in track conditions were *solely responsible* for the changes in Track Variant, but they were not significant regarding their overall effect on the horses' running times.

From the foregoing, it appears that Ruffian and Landaluce can reasonably be compared on innate ability alone regarding the times they posted in each of their juvenile races. The more obvious, extraneous factors appear to balance one another.

A Closer Look at Linear Trend Analysis

Rather than rely only on the linear trend result for the time each horse may or may not have run a given distance, we will examine only those times they actually ran for the sole distance they raced in common – six furlongs. This was also done for the colts.

Their results will be examined both with and without correction, for the impost difference that existed between them for each of their races. The reader is then invited to form his or her own opinion regarding what all this says about the horses.

Without Impost Corrections

Landaluce ran two six-furlong races during her juvenile year. She carried 117 pounds for each race. The track was rated fast for each of her races. Her times were: 68.20 s and 68.00 s.

Ruffian's two six-furlong races were also on fast-rated tracks. She carried 119 pounds for the first such race and 120 pounds for her second six-furlong race, the final of her juvenile season. Her times were 69.00 s and 68.6 s, respectively.

Thus, based on a superficial glance, Landaluce ran faster.

However, a more objective comparison should consider the impost effect. This was previously done for Colin and Man o' War using the basic formula for kinetic energy from elementary physics. That formula is, as a reminder, $KE = \frac{1}{2} \cdot mv^2$.

As discussed in chapter 4, one can use the kinetic energy formula to determine what value the velocity would have if the mass (weight carried) by a horse was changed but all other race conditions remained constant.

Using that mathematical technique, one finds that – if each of Ruffian's imposts for her six-furlong races was changed to match Landaluce's – Ruffian's average speeds for those two races would have increased such that her final times would be 68.42 s (rounding to two decimal places) and 67.74 s, respectively.

If these adjusted times are compared at six furlongs with Landaluce's times, then Ruffian's average time is 68.08 s and her standard deviation is 0.481 s for those two races.

Landaluce's average and standard deviation for her equivalent races are 68.10 s and 0.141 s, respectively.

The results suggest that the horses are about as equally matched as imaginable. Based on the preceding, we now examine the limits analysis for these races. This then concludes the final comparison between these two extraordinary fillies.

Limits Analysis: The Six-Furlong Races

The basic results of limits analysis, as applied to only the six-furlong races of Ruffian and Landaluce, are presented below. It is easily seen how adjusting Ruffian's impost slightly relative to Landaluce's makes an important difference.

Before Adjustment for Impost

	Average Time	Standard Deviation	- 3-Sigma Value
Ruffian	68.80 s	0.282 s	67.95 s
Landaluce	68.10 s	0.141 s	67.68 s

After Adjustment for Impost

	Average Time	Standard Deviation	-3-Sigma Value
Ruffian	68.08 s	0.481 s	66.63 s
Landaluce	as above	as above	as above

Naturally Landaluce's values remained the same in the second case because adjustments were to Ruffian's times only since she had the higher original imposts. It is seen that the given adjustment literally makes the difference between how the data from each horse would be interpreted by the average person, rightly or not.

Ruffian, in the case after impost adjustment, would tend to be regarded as the "better" horse, while the opposite would hold before the impost adjustment.

While a list of numerical values, as above, is useful, it does not give as dramatic an idea of what these numbers truly mean. For that, we next present the normal curves of both horses.

Limits Analysis Interpreted Via Normal Distributions

Figure 6 shows the normal distributions, after Ruffian's impost corrections, for both Ruffian and Landaluce for a typical six-furlong race.

Figure 6

Ruffian and Landaluce: Normal Curves Compared Via Limits Analysis

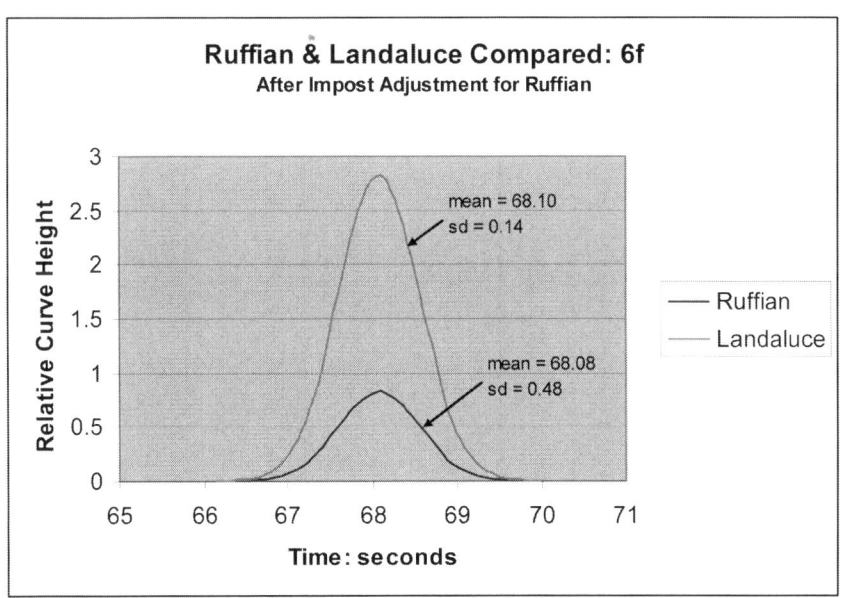

Ruffian's curve in Figure 6 was based on her mean and standard deviation after adjustment for impost. As previously mentioned, Landaluce had no adjustment since she had lower initial imposts.

Two basic methods exist, as applied to Colin's and Man o' War's data, for using limits analysis to determine how many races of one hundred each horse would be predicted to win, given the above normal distributions.

Applying the NORMDIST Function

The NORMDIST function is slower to use, but it gives excellent practice in convincing oneself that one understands the principle of how areas are distributed under normal curves.

When this method is used, it gives total areas under the curve *to the left of* the value entered as 'x' in the argument assignment for the function. Both horses' normal distributions are usually compared in three areas.

In this case the crossover points are so far out in each distribution's tail that it is impractical to break the area under the curves into three sections. One comparison area suffices.

If the area were *reasonably divisible*, one would enter the appropriate values in "NORMDIST(x, mean, standard deviation, TRUE)", as the application prompts, and Excel returns the proportion of area under the curve lying left of the value entered for x.

By then comparing the areas of both horses' distributions in the three regions, one can assign a win or loss, as appropriate, to *each unit of area* found in each region.

The present case requires modification. Areas *left of four standard deviations* and under the curves for both fillies are calculated by NORMDIST. The results are equal to within one unit in the sixth decimal place. This is so close as to be a standoff – or 'dead heat,' to slightly misuse racing lingo. It implies that if Ruffian and Landaluce ran one hundred match races of six furlongs against each other, they would virtually break even.

The second method of comparing normal curves with limits analysis is to perform a random number generation (RND function) in Excel for each horse, using the same means and standard deviations as used in the above example.

Three simulations were performed to determine how fluctuations in sampling would occur, even though the outcome is anticipated from the previous discussion.

Simulations Results

The results of the three simulations of one hundred samples each for each horse were, in terms of predicted wins:

	First Simulation	Second Simulation	Third Simulation
Ruffian:	54	53	54
Landaluce:	46	47	46

These results nicely illustrate the vagaries of random sampling – even from known distributions. They also highlight why it is virtually impossible to determine or predict the likely outcome of any race in real life.

There are simply too many factors entering the sampling process for a high prediction level, unless, of course, one horse is so superior to another that their data clearly show it.

This certainly is not the present case. Based on the above discussion, one would be hard pressed to state that either horse was "better," particularly for running a distance of six furlongs.

Other distances must be similarly checked, but that is virtually prohibited since these horses shared no other common running distances.

Therefore, if a stranger approached you and simply stated "Ruffian was a better two-year-old than Landaluce," you could immediately and fearlessly reply, "At what?"

Unfortunately, most people compare horses at only the gut-level of consideration. They like the horse for some reason, and they'll be damned if anyone is going to disparage in any manner something they like, whether the challenge is logical or not!

That is the way of human nature, pure and simple. Dare we add, the way of all flesh?

A Year Later and Foolish Pleasure

Anyone remotely familiar with thoroughbred racing knows the tragic story of the match race between Ruffian and Foolish Pleasure. It occurred at Belmont Park on Sunday, July 6, 1975 and was a ten-furlong event – the Kentucky Derby distance.

Ruffian broke down, and the injuries ultimately cost her life because she could not be calmed after coming out of surgery.

Since this book highlights the juvenile seasons only of these four special thoroughbreds, it is not the place to describe the Ruffian-Foolish Pleasure match in detail.

However, it is not remiss to state how these two champions performed as juveniles and what that might have portended for their match race, had it occurred without mishap.

Foolish Pleasure raced seven times as a juvenile. He ran at distances from five furlongs to one mile. He carried between 116 pounds and 122 pounds in these races. All were on tracks rated fast except for two. Those were run on tracks rated good. Therefore, deriving a linear trend for Foolish Pleasure should give reasonably accurate estimations of how he would have run the same distances as Ruffian.

Foolish Pleasure's linear trend is expressed as:

$$\hat{y} = 97.31x - 2.12$$

His COD is 0.9969, and his standard error of the mean is 0.736 s.

As for most thoroughbreds studied, the COD has an extremely high value. It indicates that the linear trend fits the data with nearly 99.7 percent accuracy.

Using the above equation and setting x equal to 0.75 miles (the distance Ruffian raced most often), one finds that the predicted time for Foolish Pleasure is 70.86 seconds.

It is inappropriate to adjust Foolish Pleasure's imposts to match Ruffian's since colts are naturally expected to carry more weight. The actual average impost Foolish Pleasure carried in his seven races was 120.29 pounds. This is approximately just two pounds more than Ruffian's average impost, and cannot justify modification, considering the expectations between fillies and colts.

We see from the linear trends of both horses that Ruffian's predicted time for six furlongs is 68.80 seconds and that she averaged, therefore, as a juvenile, 2.06 s faster at the distance than did Foolish Pleasure. Hence, she needed no impost adjustment.

This is a large enough time difference for the distance that one need not compare the horses via limits analysis. Ruffian is predicted to win 99 of 100 match races at six furlongs – using a single RND simulation based on their linear trend data.

This is sufficient to state that, all other factors in their development being equal, Ruffian would have had an extremely good chance of beating Foolish Pleasure as a sophomore, had the race been successfully completed. She was leading by about three quarters of a length near the three-quarter pole when her breakdown occurred.

Returning now to the fillies, an objective assessment of the data shows that Landaluce was, in all likelihood, equivalent to Ruffian as a two-year-old. Her untimely death prevented what probably could have been a match similarly electrifying to those of Affirmed and Alydar, but for the age discrepancy which would have prohibited it.

Ruffian was listed by Blood-Horse Magazine in 1999 as thirty-fifth best of one-hundred champion Thoroughbreds of the 20th Century. In my opinion, that rating was too low.

Also in my opinion, Landaluce deserved at least a ranking within the Blood-Horse top one hundred. She is not, however, mentioned.

But mature adults realize that life is seldom fair. The Fates moved their collective heads negatively, and the brilliant Landaluce was forgotten by many. *Sic Transit Gloria Mundi.*

It is time now to discuss the horses which deserve at least honorable mention when compared to the principal four horses featured herein.

Paradoxically, chance lies at the root of most of the uniformities of the world we are familiar with. Complete chaos possesses statistical uniformities.
-- John D. Barrow

CHAPTER 8

Five Thoroughbreds Honorably Mentioned

To this point, concentration was focused mainly on four unquestionably great thoroughbreds. Chronologically, by racing years, they were Colin, Man o' War, Ruffian and Landaluce. Thus, the lives and track accomplishments of two colts and two fillies were emphasized.

It would be remiss, however, not to mention five additional outstanding juvenile racers. These five horses (using the generic term for brevity) are not the prime focus of this work for separate reasons which will be explained briefly as the horses are introduced. Those reasons by no means indicate that they are not also 'beyond greatness.' It means only that other mitigating circumstances influenced the propriety of their equivalent presentation herein.

As mentioned earlier, the colts Sysonby and Secretariat and the fillies First Flight, La Prevoyante and Personal Ensign are the remaining outstanding juvenile runners whose accomplishments this chapter briefly examines.

Sysonby
(1902 – 1906)

Sysonby (pronounced: SY-sun-bee) was the true chronological harbinger of thoroughbred greatness for the 20th Century. He was named for a hunting lodge in the English town of Melton Mowbray by Foxhall Keene, son of Sysonby's breeder, James R. Keene.

Sysonby was sired by Melton, winner of the 1885 Epsom Derby. His dam was Optime, granddaughter of the unbeaten Ormonde.

As a juvenile, Sysonby entered six races and won five. It was proven that he was administered the drug bromeliad just before his fifth race, in which he finished third by five lengths.

That was his only loss in two seasons of racing. His career record for fifteen races was fourteen wins, of which thirteen were stakes races, and the singular, disputed third place, also a stakes race.

His solitary juvenile loss was the only reason for not including Sysonby with Colin and Man o' War in this study. Even though he *probably* would have won the race, this still assumes an outcome that was not in question for the four primary horses studied herein. A similar reason holds for Secretariat. Although Man o' War also lost once as a juvenile, he would have beaten Upset, had one stride remained before the wire.

However, that fact aside, it is obvious from the times he posted – probably on slower tracks than Colin encountered, and certainly slower than tracks run on by Man o' War – that Sysonby could have held his own with either of these colts. The times for Sysonby, Colin and Man o' War for only their six-furlong races – all run on tracks rated fast – are shown below for comparison. All three horses had more races at this common distance than at others, and it is therefore judged the best distance for comparison. It is, in fact, probably a kind of modal distance for juveniles.

By contrasting their times (in seconds) for fast tracks only, some disparity between their data is eliminated. Correcting for major factors, as was done for Colin and Man o' War can never eliminate all the influences that affected a given horse in a given race, and so it is the better part of discretion to leave it at that.

Time Comparisons

Sysonby	Colin	Man o' War
19Sep04 Gra: 69.60	7Oct07 Bel: 72.00	13Sep19 Bel: 71.60
16Jul04 Bri: 73.00	31Aug07 She: 71.20	23Aug19 Sar: 72.00
	14Aug07 Sar: 73.00	2Aug19 Sar: 72.40
	27Jul07 Bri: 72.20	5Jul19 Aqu: 73.00

The track abbreviations above are: Gra = Gravesend, NY; Bri = Brighton Beach, NY; Bel = Belmont Park, NY; She = Sheepshead Bay, NY; Sar = Saratoga Springs, NY; Aqu = Aqueduct, NY.

Sysonby's times for six furlongs compare well indeed with those of Colin and Man o' War. In fact, his 69.60 seconds at Gravesend, NY is easily the fastest time at that distance of the three horses. Sysonby ran a third six-furlong race, but it was the one in which he was given the drug that undoubtedly cost him a win.

It is likely that, given the fact he preceded Colin by three years, Sysonby ran on slower tracks. It is certain that, given the discussion in chapter 4 on track improvements at both Belmont Park and Saratoga, he ran on slower tracks than did Man o' War.

Sysonby's slowest six furlongs, in the time of 73.00 seconds, is, in fact, the same as the slowest times for that distance by both Colin and Man o' War.

Given even this cursory look at Sysonby's juvenile data, one would be hard pressed to declare that he was not as fast as either Colin or Man o' War.

Sysonby ran only two juvenile distances, five-and-a-half and six furlongs. Man o' War ran those same distances in eight juvenile races plus five furlongs in two others. However, in Sysonby's case his linear trend does not have as high a COD as either Man o' War's or Colin's. Sysonby's COD is 0.8059. Data scatter and paucity are probably the causes.

This means that about eighty-one percent of Sysonby's run times are predictable from his distances. This COD is lower than for nearly any other thoroughbred studied. This lower COD, plus its concomitantly less reliable prediction level, are the other factors keeping Sysonby from being unquestionably ranked with the four primary horses in this study.

Secretariat
(1970 – 1989)

By any standard on any planet, Secretariat would indisputably rank with the greatest thoroughbreds ever to race. That he is not included as a primary colt in this study hinges on two reasons.

First, ambiguous as the term 'era' is, Secretariat would undoubtedly qualify as being from another era than either Colin or Man o' War.

The second reason is the same as for Sysonby. As great as he was, Secretariat lost one juvenile race, his maiden at Aqueduct. Since he was badly bumped exiting the gate, one could argue his case. Other than that, he ran spotlessly in eight of nine races.

Although he had good reason for losing his maiden effort at Aqueduct, we will attribute that to the same bad luck suffered by many horses, alluded to by Hollingsworth (5), and will not count his juvenile year as 'perfect' as were the corresponding years for Colin or Man o' War, despite the latter's single loss.

Considering that he was nearly knocked down, Secretariat nonetheless finished that race in fourth place, just one and one-half lengths off the lead – and it was only a five and one-half furlong event. Needless to say, his recovery effort at the short distance greatly impressed all those watching who remotely understood racing talent.

It certainly is, however, entirely appropriate to comment briefly on his ability, regardless of what his slightly blemished juvenile year may otherwise suggest.

Juvenile Linear Trend Analysis

When a linear trend is calculated using Excel for Secretariat's juvenile races – excluding the ill-fated maiden effort for which it cannot be fairly said that the final time truly represents his ability – the following equation results:

$$\hat{y} = 104.98x – 8.58$$

As a reminder, ŷ represents the predicted time that Secretariat would run a given distance, x. The value 104.98 is the slope of his linear trend line, while -8.58 is its intercept with the y axis (the vertical time axis). All values in the equation are rounded to two decimal places, as typically done throughout this study.

Especially note that Secretariat's associated *coefficient of determination* is 0.9967 and his standard error of the mean is 0.918 s. The former number indicates how well the linear trend fits his data (extremely well), while the standard error of the mean of Excel's LINEST function is essentially the standard deviation that can be expected around any predicted value.

Using this equation, Secretariat's predicted times (in seconds) for the four standard juvenile distances he ran, excluding the maiden race distance, are:

0.75 miles	0.8125 miles	1.00 miles	1.0625 miles
70.15	76.71	96.40	102.96

Since one could claim an era effect regarding Secretariat relative to Colin or Man o' War, we can simply contrast his times as a juvenile with those of the former two horses and concede that some adjustments of Secretariat's times are probably necessary (but not easily determined) before comparing him with the runners of earlier decades. Further elaboration of this point is unnecessary.

However, the corresponding six-furlong times for both Colin and Man o' War are displayed below, since that is the only common distance the three colts shared.

Colin	Man o' War
0.75 miles	0.75 miles
71.44 s	72.19 s

Colin's time is the adjusted time determined in chapter 4 to account for the slower tracks on which he ran compared with Man o' War.

It is left for the reader to form his or her own opinion about whether the time differences between Secretariat and the other two colts at six furlongs could reasonably be attributed to some combination of track condition and steel racing plates **from another era**. A partial answer to this is given in chapter 10.

It should also be noted, preparatory to any such analysis, that one of the two races Secretariat ran at eight and a-half furlongs was on a track rated 'sloppy.'

Interestingly, he ran that race in 102.80 s at Laurel Racetrack. His other race of equal length was on a track rated 'fast,' and he ran that in 104.40 s. He therefore ran distinctly slower on the *faster rated* track – contrary to what many self-proclaimed racing pundits would argue.

Thus, true to what his jockey, Ron Turcotte, once observed, surface conditions didn't matter to Secretariat. He ran well under any conditions! Additionally, Turcotte undoubtedly didn't need to push Secretariat on the faster tracks, and so he did not.

Secretariat won both races. He won by three and one-half lengths on the fast track – that win being described as 'handily.' He won on the slower track by eight lengths. His performance line described that win as 'easily.' Go figure!

We turn now to three fillies most deserving the honorable mention denied them to this point.

First Flight, La Prevoyante and Personal Ensign are discussed, as in previous cases, in their chronological racing order throughout the twentieth century.

First Flight
(1944 – 1973)

First Flight was a brown filly foaled in 1944. She was by Mahmoud out of Fly Swatter. In a career spanning three years, she ran twenty-four times. Her overall record was 11-3-3.

Although her total record is not stellar, her juvenile year was among the very best a filly ever ran. She lost just once out of six races, while running distances from four and one-half to six and one-half furlongs during 1946.

In fact, she generally turned in blazing times, considering that she was supposedly hampered by two banes of her era - steel plates and slower tracks. All six of her juvenile races were at Belmont Park from May 7 through October 5.

If one compares the speeds at Belmont Park during the decade of the forties with those of an equivalent race in the decades of the late sixties through the mid seventies, a decent estimate of how much correction for track surface can justly be made in her case is obtained. The Futurity qualifies for this purpose.

The Futurity was a six and one-half furlong race when run by First Flight in 1946. In fact, it was run on the Widener Course at Belmont from 1926 until 1958. However, it was run at six and one-half furlongs only from 1934 to 1975, according to the American Racing Manual 2005 (8).

These years suffice to compare the average running times of the Futurity during the decade of the forties with those of the years 1968 through 1975. These latter years include Secretariat's 1972 victory. We are, therefore, given a good chance to make an unbiased comparison of the track surfaces for both First Flight's and Secretariat's races.

Finding the Unexpected

A slightly embarrassing fact now emerges for those claiming that horses from earlier generations *invariably* faced slower tracks than did more 'modern' horses.

When the Futurity data for the two sets of years are compared, we find the average running time for that race during the decade of the forties was 1.01 seconds **faster** than the average running time for the years 1968 through 1975.

The former average is 75.94 s while the latter average is 76.95 s. Isn't that strange?

Obviously, in light of this fact, one cannot realistically assume that the Belmont Park track surface was slower throughout the 1940s than it was from 1968 to 1975.

Now a perplexed or disgruntled reader might object that the weights carried between the two eras were *entirely different*. That, however, would be arguing erroneously as the following facts taken from the American Racing Manual 2005 disclose.

When the numbers are checked, it happens that each horse in the years 1968 through 1975 bore a 122-pound impost. There was no impost variation in that time period. However, the winning horses throughout the 1940s ran under imposts ranging from 119 pounds to 126 pounds – the average impost for the ten years being 123.50 pounds. This is another contradictory, and rather surprising, disclosure.

The preceding means that, not only did the earlier era horses shoulder more average weight – they also ran the race in a significantly faster average time.

In fact, the difference in average running times for the two sets of data gives a t value of 0.014. This is definitely significant. It implies that there are *only fourteen chances in one thousand* that this difference is due to coincidence or sampling error.

The t test value for the difference in average imposts for the two eras is 0.069. This is a level which statisticians generally consider *not significant*, being higher than the significance level of 0.05 considered necessary to show a true difference between samples. The two sets of imposts must thus be considered equivalent.

A Suggested Interpretation

The obvious conclusion, thus, is that First Flight – forgotten now to the extent that standard thoroughbred sources do not even include her death date [it was located by Mr. Allan Carter, historian of the National Museum of Thoroughbred Racing in the stud books (15)]– convincingly ran six and one-half furlongs faster than did Secretariat. Unfortunately, a direct comparison cannot be made for the four major champions highlighted in this study because none ran that same distance as a juvenile.

However, from their linear trends, a very good estimate of their times for six and one-half furlongs can be derived, and these are presented below, for the fillies only, as a convenient reference and comparison. All time units are in seconds.

Ruffian: 74.67

Landaluce: 74.94

First Flight: 75.20 actual; 74.88 projected from linear trend

One is hard pressed, considering the extremely small sample size upon which these estimates are based, to say that any of these fillies was not the equivalent of the others – at this particular distance and during their juvenile years as runners.

La Prevoyante
(1970 – 1974)

La Prevoyante was a brown filly foaled in 1970, the same year as Secretariat. She was Canadian. Her sire was Buckpasser and her dam was Arctic Dancer.

Equine author Richard Sowers summed up her somewhat inconsistent career (10) by noting that she is one of only two fillies to win five major races as a juvenile but that never again won a major stakes race.

Her juvenile record was, in fact, spotless. She ran twelve times and won all twelve. For the remaining twenty-seven of her career races, she won thirteen, placed in five and showed three times. This made her career record 25-5-3 out of thirty-nine starts. This is still an excellent resume.

She is included herein on the merits of her exemplary juvenile season of 1972.

The predicted values for five standard distances, as derived from individual linear trend analyses, are given below for Landaluce, La Prevoyante, Ruffian and First Flight. Although such values are always subject to the standard error of estimate, in the present cases they give very good approximations to the relative abilities of the four fillies, especially since their coefficients of determination are all well above 0.99.

Comparison Times: Four Top Fillies

	0.6875	0.75	0.875	1.00	1.0625
Landaluce	61.37	68.15	81.72	95.29	102.08

La Prevoyante	64.94	71.78	85.45	99.12	105.96
Ruffian	62.93	68.80	**80.53**	**92.27**	**98.13**
First Flight	63.20	69.04	80.72	92.41	98.25

Note that the fastest predicted times at each distance are in bold font. Note also that the times for one mile, both for Ruffian and for First Flight – despite the presumed era differences she may have faced - are nearly equal to Dr. Fager's 1968 world record, which still stands. That surrealistic time was 92.20 seconds.

Recall, however, that Dr. Fager was assigned an enormous impost for that race – 134 pounds. Still, the ability of the fillies remains stellar, Dr. Fager's nearly freakish talent for running under heavy and even absurd burdens notwithstanding.

From the above, one must conclude that First Flight compares extremely favorably with either Landaluce or Ruffian, especially considering that compensation was not made for track effects but just for the fact that she wore steel plates. Those plates add approximately two additional pounds to the stated impost of all horses from earlier in the past century. At minimum, they make a difference of at least 0.30 s at distances approaching ten furlongs, as can be calculated using the KE formula.

La Prevoyante was fated to suffer a ruptured lung shortly after her final race of Saturday, December 28, 1974. That was the mile and one-sixteenth Miss Florida Handicap held at Calder Race Course. That lethal condition is undoubtedly what caused her to finish eighth by five and three-quarters lengths.

La Prevoyante was voted into the Canadian Horse Racing Hall of Fame in 1976. In 1995 she was inducted into the U.S. National Museum of Racing Hall of Fame.

She was a great champion and deserves due recognition by all those fancying even a modest knowledge of thoroughbred racing ability.

Personal Ensign
(1984 – 2010)

The filly Personal Ensign was born on April 27, 1984 – also the author's birth anniversary, albeit some years later.

She had a perfect career spanning three years, 1986 through 1988. Her final record for thirteen starts was: 13-0-0. Of those thirteen victories, ten were in stakes races. She is the only Thoroughbred of the 'modern' era to race undefeated since Colin. In twelve of her races, she won by an average margin of 4.66 lengths.

She is obviously included in this study based on her undefeated juvenile season.

Data Limitations

The primary reason for not granting her equal status with Landaluce and Ruffian is that she raced only twice in her juvenile year. The distances she ran were seven furlongs and one mile, both at Belmont Park.

Since a perfect straight line is always assured by only two data points, linear trend analysis for her juvenile season is pointless – literally, and as a pun. The results would naturally show a coefficient of determination equaling 1.00, and she would have no standard error of the mean associated with her trend line.

This would not allow reliable time estimates for her various distances, since it is unrealistic to attribute zero standard error to real-world data.

Had she raced but one additional time, it would have tipped the balance just enough that a complete trend line could be calculated for her, albeit a shaky one.

Her single effort at one mile, on a fast track, yielded a time of 96.40 seconds. This is not as fast as the similar times at the distance for Landaluce, Ruffian or First Flight. However, it is unfair to make a direct comparison based solely on this single number.

Therefore, we must turn from further such comparisons, satisfied that her career overall certainly entitles her to be honorably mentioned in this study.

One must ask, however, how she could not have been exception-ally gifted as a runner. When her pedigree is even cursorily reviewed, one finds the following great champions amongst her forebears, all within just four generations of her sire and dam: Damascus, Sword Dancer, Buckpasser, Tom Fool, Swaps, Hoist the Flag, Tom Rolfe and War Admiral.

That list should have been, in fact, sufficient to assure her unique-ness. But genetics doesn't always 'Darwinize' as it is theorized.

Personal Ensign was elected to the U.S. National Museum of Racing Hall of Fame in 1993. In 1999 the Blood-Horse Magazine staff of seven racing authorities voted her number forty-eight in the top one hundred Thoroughbreds of the 20th Century. I believe that ranking errs slightly this side of modesty.

Personal Ensign lived a substantial lifespan for her species. She died, aged twenty-six, in early April of 2010.

I returned, and saw under the sun, that the race is not to the swift, nor the battle to the strong . . . ; but time and chance happeneth to them all.
- - Ecclesiastes 9:11

CHAPTER 9

The Question of Thoroughbred Greatness

Suppose there were two thoroughbred horses having perfect records. Assume that one was a filly and the other a colt. Further imagine that they each ran twelve races in each of their juvenile and sophomore seasons. They then retired.

Carry this imagining even further and say that they ran the entire gamut of standard distances for each of those years and each ran the identical time for identical distances.

Now go even further into fantasy. Assume they were born a year apart. Thus, they didn't compete directly with each other. However, the filly – born a year before the colt – won both the Filly Triple Crown and the 'regular' Triple Crown as a sophomore.

To make all this comparison even more fantastic, suppose the colt also won the regular Triple Crown during his sophomore season.

Nothing was different about these unbelievable creatures except that the filly carried less weight, about three pounds per race, than the colt.

All their races were run on the same tracks and all under fast conditions – at least rated fast for their particular races.

All this begs the question – which horse (again, using the simpler generic name for an equine) was greater? Were they identical since their results were absolutely identical – other, naturally, than that the colt could not qualify to run in the Filly Triple Crown (the Triple Tiara) events?

You might immediately object that the filly had an advantage due to lighter imposts. However, only a die-hard quibbler would do this under these conditions. And besides, there is no consistent correlation between impost and running time, especially considering the rather slim three-pound difference for this case. So let us agree to dismiss impost differential as a valid determiner of equality regarding greatness.

The truth is that greatness, in an absolute philosophical sense, cannot be defined. It is an inherent quality of a person or creature that is some combination of genetic endowment and development – aided by nurture, if you will.

It is similar to the concept of human intelligence in this regard. Nearly every sane person would agree that something called intelligence exists within humans. And it probably can be further agreed that it resides in or is produced by some interaction of the material brain and electro-chemical currents within that brain.

It is, in other words, some product of what is called the mind-brain interaction within the human species.

All this sounds fine and appropriately academic, but it still proves nothing about the nature of intelligence. Nor does it say whether intelligence, posited as existing and suggested by various talents and abilities, can actually be quantified.

Many psychological observers and experimenters used to think that intelligence could be and actually was 'measured' by so-called intelligence tests. However, that is logic based on circular reasoning.

One cannot get by any more in savvy company by saying that intelligence is what intelligence tests measure. Such is considered circular reasoning – using the term to be defined within the definition. Many theologians have been and remain adept at it.

Neither can inherent greatness be quantified – in horses or in any other sentient beings one cares to imagine.

What then remains to argue about regarding the relative merits of thoroughbreds?

All we can say is that we can analyze the times and distances that various running horses have left us. We can say that these hint at or are even some sort of product of their inherent greatness, but that is all we can say.

Past performance records show *what* happened. They contain facts about races. They do not enable people to look deep inside the creature and say that one horse has a certain amount more or less of greatness than another simply by virtue of his or her performance records. They remind us somewhat of Plato's famous Cave Allegory in this regard – we observers are like creatures in a cave watching a parade of shadows on the wall, produced by an exterior light which we can never directly inspect. (16)

There are simply too many random factors influencing the outcome of individual races to say that all a creature possessed as a runner was enabled to show on a given day.

For that to be a valid judgment would be equivalent to saying that the horse ran at least at or below its negative three-sigma level. The probability of that happening is, assuming an approximately normal distribution of run times, 0.135 percent.

The number 0.135 is the fractional area under a normal distribution equal to or less than the negative three-sigma (i.e., minus three standard deviations) level.

The probability is at least that low that a given horse runs at the highest average speed of which it is capable at a given distance and on a particular day.

This reasoning refers, of course, only to one race. Saying that a horse even approached showing its inherent talent or 'greatness' for a season implies that it ran at that same level *for each race* in the given season.

Therefore, if the horse in question had twelve total races for the season, then one must raise 0.135 to the twelfth power to determine the probability of the horse showing its *absolute full* potential – what I would closely equate to true greatness. This is equivalent to 0.135 multiplied by itself twelve times, or $(0.135)^{12}$.

The result is an astronomically low probability. In scientific and decimal notation, respectively, it is: 3.664E-11 and 0.00000000003664. Upon taking the reciprocal of that number (i.e., 1 divided by the number) we find that the odds reduce to about one in 27.29 billion. That's low enough to qualify as slim and none in most books!

For readers having scant feeling for such numbers, this probability is essentially equivalent to the odds of tossing an honest coin thirty-five consecutive times and having either all tails or all heads show. Actually, the more exact calculation makes the answer between thirty-four and thirty-five coin tosses. However, a fractional coin toss is akin to being partially pregnant – unrealistic. And so I rounded up.

Thus, when one applies statistics to analyze and compare racing data, one is merely applying the best possible *factual* analysis. One is not discerning the creature's *absolute worth*. To think otherwise is to totally misunderstand what human measurement is about or of what it is capable.

Considering the above, nobody who has walked upon earth actually knows how great Sysonby, Colin, Man o' War, Secretariat or any other horse was.

But let us leave this topic and go now to a related one, the concept of eras and not being able to compare horses from those different, perhaps imagined, time fragments.

The Era Roadblock

More people than one can imagine have such a deep psychological investment in certain horses from bygone days that they absolutely will contrive whatever argument seems capable of proving them correct regarding that horse's worth.

Their perpetual cry is, "You can't compare horses from different eras!" Although this theme was touched upon earlier, it is proper to examine it in more detail and from a different angle than previously. In fact, I'll summarize yet another view on this question in the following and final chapter.

I do not remotely think that any argument will convince people of this mindset to reconsider their predilections. However, I wish to clarify just what the hue and cry is all about and to examine whether it is a valid cacophony.

First, we note almost immediately that these protesters soon violate their own principle or dictum. They no more than utter their tiresome mantra than they exclaim something like, "But we know that Horse A was better than Horse B."

That is a direct comparison, pure and simple. It is unadorned with any supporting evidence, to be sure. But it is nonetheless a comparison. Strike one against this adversary of 'comparative equine excellence.'

Second, they would be hard pressed, if truly challenged, to define what an era implies regarding thoroughbred racing.

They generally mean sometime early in the 20th Century as opposed to late in the same century, but they cannot delimit measurable boundaries for this land of the forbidden fruit. Strike two!

Now there is a general rule within science that if a tentative truth, generally termed a hypothesis, meets a single instance of disproof, it is no longer considered a viable candidate for the title "Law of Science."

Any time-honored law of science must first pass this stringent test of not being refuted – not even once! It applies to Einstein's general relativity as it does to the laws of thermodynamics and to any principle elevated to the status of law that you care to name.

Given this hard fact, we have already shown earlier that the average running times for the Futurity at Belmont Park were actually *lower* between 1940 and 1950 than they were from 1968 through 1975. This is, therefore, a disconfirming instance of the idea implicit in not making era comparisons – that tracks were, *a priori*, slower earlier in the past century than in later years. Thus, horses running these slower tracks were forced into lower speeds.

If one such contradictory instance can be found with so little effort, there are no doubt numerous other supporting cases of this same phenomenon.

Tracks from older times may have been – **but were not necessarily** – significantly slower than tracks from times closer to the present. Strike three!

There is a tendency to forget that another factor besides track surface enters into this judgment. It is the concept of foal crop. This topic was discussed thoroughly in GHA. Evidence was presented therein that the size of the foal crop into which a horse is born can strongly influence the average decade running times of races he or she will enter – to the extent that foal crop size may account for at least eighty percent of differences in running times.

Mathematical trends of this nature were explained and examined carefully for several major tracks in this regard. Those tracks included Churchill Downs, Pimlico, Belmont Park and Santa Anita. The trend of faster running times across decades of the 20th Century with increases in foal crop was shown to be a highly feasible possibility.

It was not shown with absolute certainty, because statistics can never show things on that level. However, the trend was strong enough to cast doubt on the supposition that track surface was solely responsible for faster or slower times.

A Genetic Approach

Let's take a slightly different look at the premise that horses from different eras can't be accurately compared.

The entire purpose of selective breeding within the thoroughbred bloodlines is to obtain horses of greater running ability. This applies to both speed and stamina. In other words, breeding is manipulated with both the hope and the intention that the right genes from the sire and dam of a given foal will interact to produce the maximum combination of speed and stamina reasonable within this particular species.

Using the name Man o' War simply because he is the focus of much of the protest in the era argument, one must realize that he was foaled in 1917. Then ask whether it is reasonable, in light of the selective breeding purpose stated above, to expect that a single horse from earlier in the past century would – for all time and in all ways – be superior to horses coming after him?

If that principle were true, then one may as well stop breeding and wrap up thoroughbred racing, because it has already produced the best it can.

However, I do not believe that is true. The past performance re-cords of numerous runners indicate that, even if it were only for certain distances, they were almost undoubtedly faster than Man o' War. The names Sysonby and Colin spring to mind in this regard.

But let us not get carried away with suppositions. There is, in fact, a very simple statistical device that can be used to compare horses from different eras. And it does not depend one bit on track conditions or on any other single factor operative during the era. It depends only upon the relative standing of a given horse among his or her peers.

In fact, when the test was performed on data from both Man o' War's and Secretariat's past performance charts, it was found that Secretariat ranked slightly higher among his peers than Man o' War did relative to his.

The technique of this z-score, as it is known within statistics, will now be explained.

Determining Relative Status Among Peers: No Era Effect Involved

Although the theme of this book is the juvenile racing year, data were taken from the three-year-old past performance records of both Man o' War and Secretariat for better comparison. The reason is primar-ily that more complete sophomore-year data are available for each horse. All data are from the American Racing Manual 2005 (8).

As three-year-olds, Man o' War ran eleven times and Secretariat ran twelve times. The most statistically similar sophomore data exist for seven of Man o' War's eleven races and for nine of Secretariat's twelve races.

The objective is to find those races in which the distances *and* the tracks on which each colt ran stayed relatively constant for the greatest number of consecutive years.

Many races change venues surprisingly often, as the American Racing Manual 2005 indicates – via an extended footnote at the end of each of its data compilations for a particular event.

For example, the Belmont was first run in 1867. However, it was not held at Belmont Park, and it was not twelve furlongs. In fact, it was thirteen furlongs from 1867 through 1873 and it was run at Jerome Park from 1867 until 1890. It has also been run at Aqueduct and at Morris Park, and its distances have jumped from thirteen furlongs to ten furlongs to nine furlongs to eleven furlongs and, last, to the present familiar value of twelve furlongs. It has been a kind of study in racing saltation, if you will. (8)

It was, in fact, eleven furlongs in 1920 when Man o' War ran it.

Numerous races change tracks and distances throughout their running history. Therefore, those races of both Man o' War and Secretariat were chosen which seemed to hold their consistency for both length and track location for the greatest number of *consecutive years preceding and following* the years each of these horses ran them.

Of the seven races chosen for Man o' War, the average number of years *before* he ran and for which the race was at the same track and at the same distance was seven. Thus, on average, data were taken for the year of each race in which he ran beginning at the year 1913.

Of the same seven races, the average number of years *after* Man o' War ran them and for which the data was correlated for both same distance and same track conditions was 6.7. This basically means that data up to and including 1927, seven years after Man o' War ran the same race, were obtained.

For Secretariat's nine races, the average number of years *before* he ran and for which consistent data were obtained was 8.7. This implies that data back to 1964 were used. On the other end, the average number of years for same-distance and same-track conditions *after* he ran was 8.2. This implies that roughly the year 1981 was the final year of data included to rank Secretariat against his peers for those particular races.

The z-score is easily computed. It is, fortunately, simpler than the explanation. The average of the running times for the years *surrounding the year* in which the given horse ran is subtracted from the running time for the given horse, either Man o' War or Secretariat in this case. That result is then *divided by the standard deviation* of the running times for the entire set of those same surrounding years for that particular race.

The result, therefore, directly shows by *how many standard deviations* the given horse's running time differs from the *average running time* for the same race for those years selected on either side of the given horse's race year.

Since the explanation needed length for clarity, an example is in order. One from Man o' War's 1920 Travers is selected.

In 1920 Man o' War ran the Travers at ten furlongs in 121.80 seconds. For the years 1910 through 1930, the Travers was at the same distance and was held at the same track, Saratoga. Additional years could have been used for this race, but in this case the sample was considered large enough to give an accurate z score.

The average running time for the Travers during those years was 126.43 s. The standard deviation for the same years was 3.236 s. When the average running time is *subtracted from* Man o' War's time the result is 121.80 – 126.43, or - 4.63 s. When -4.63 is divided by the standard deviation, 3.236, the result is -1.43.

That result, -1.43, is Man o' War's z-score for that particular span of race years compared with the results of his peers. It can be safely assumed that the years from 1910 through 1930 [no Travers was run in 1911 or 1912 (8)] are within the same era, since absolutely nobody can define the boundaries of a horseracing era to begin with.

Thus, Man o' War ran the Travers at a level that was better than all his peers by about 1.4 standard deviations, as the minus sign indicates.

The same method and formula was used for the other comparison races of both Man o' War and Secretariat.

The race names and z-scores for each horse are listed below for complete reference. Man o' War's sophomore races were in 1920 and Secretariat's were in 1973.

Comparisons: Man o' War, Secretariat and z-scores for sophomore years

Man o' War		Secretariat	
Race	**z score**	**Race**	**z score**
Preakness	-1.202	Bayshore	-0.047

Withers	-1.836	Gotham	-1.661
Belmont	-2.218	Wood Memorial	0.898
Stuyvesant	1.839	Kentucky Derby	-2.372
Dwyer	-0.966	Preakness	-1.901
Travers	-1.431	Belmont	-2.660
Lawrence	-0.613	Whitney	0.551
		Marlboro	-1.339
		Man o' War	-1.293

The average z-score for Man o' War for his seven races is -0.918. The average z- score for Secretariat's nine races is -1.092. A t test between the two sets of z scores shows *no significant difference* between the two horses. The t value is 0.7944, to four decimal places.

This implies that a nearly 80-percent chance exists (79.44 percent to be more technical) that the two sets of z scores could have been randomly selected from the same population of scores. That is considered a very high probability level in statistics.

Thus, both horses essentially rank equal among their peers approximately eight years on either side of the year in which each ran their particular races.

Based on the above, can Man o' War and Secretariat be considered equivalent? That question still remains moot. The logical tendency should be to say that Secretariat faced more and stiffer competition when he raced than did Man o' War.

About fifty years of selective breeding would be argued to have produced more potentially great runners in the larger foal crop Secretariat faced than did that from which Man o' War's competition came.

These foal crop figures are presented below. It is left for the reader's judgment to determine whether, in fact, Secretariat faced stiffer competition per race than did Man o' War. I believe that point is, at best, only marginally arguable.

This is not a poorly disguised attempt to denigrate or enhance the record of either horse. It is a concomitant of the facts of thoroughbred breeding across time's passing.

According to an excerpt from the Jockey Club Fact Book (17), the foal crop for Man o' War's birth year of 1917 was 1,680. The foal crop for Secretariat's birth year of 1970 was 24,361.

If we accept Hollingsworth's comment (18) that only 2.5 percent of a given foal crop are destined to win even one stakes race, then the relative true competition figures for those two foal crops are 42 and 609, respectively.

This makes it obvious that Secretariat would have had a greater chance of facing more qualified competition per race than did Man o' War. However, it does not prove that he did.

If we assume that they both faced equal competition across the years of their z- score comparisons, then the results already presented say that the two horses should be judged as equivalent to their peers and, therefore, to each other. Neither was better.

A final word in this chapter on possible standardization for measuring the speeds of track surfaces follows. The following chapter gives a summary follow-up to the statistical definition of greatness presented in chapter 8. And that will close this study related to equine greatness on the racing track.

A Possible Track Speed Measurement Device

It would be tremendously helpful, especially toward solving the era and comparison issues, if a governing body such as the National Thoroughbred Racing Association would sponsor the development of a scientific track-speed measuring device.

The following is offered as a preliminary suggestion. Admittedly, I do not know whether a standard measure of various track surfaces is possible. It should be in principle. Mr. Spock would have undoubtedly suggested that it was theoretically possible. However, with minimal expense for development and testing, one would know once and for all whether this often bellicose issue might be settled.

A Test Machine or Robot

It is certainly possible to develop a device, I envision it something like a standard riding lawn mower, which would be remote-controlled and designed to run along a test strip made to simulate track conditions from decades past.

If the formulas for the composition and construction methods of at least some major tracks are still available, as I would guess they are in dark and hallowed archival vaults, then a test strip – perhaps a furlong in length – could be made over which the test vehicle or robot could run.

One would need to insure that its engine speed was held constant, or within close tolerances, from trial to trial. That should suffice to guarantee that only track resistance determined whether it would run faster or slower. It should probably be given a minimal length in which to attain maximum speed before entering the test strip – for example, on a relatively short asphalt approach.

That maximum robot speed would be best which was about in the mid to top range of typical racing speeds – perhaps about 55 ft/s, or 37.5 miles per hour. This is certainly an attainable goal.

If reality approximates theory, it is reasonable to think that this device would slow by varying degrees, even though the engine speed remained nearly constant, as it traversed different test surfaces. Perhaps it should be named 'Travers'?

Nonetheless, by measuring the relative times it took to cover the same distance over two different surfaces, a meaningful correlation might be obtained on how changes in the robot's speed and time corresponded to effects on a horse running the same surfaces.

Suppose, for example, one such furlong-length test surface was made to duplicate that of Belmont Park's in 1917. From an earlier discussion, we know that 1917 was the year before a major improvement in the Belmont Park racing surface was made.

Further suppose that when the test robot ran on both the reconstructed older surface and on a strip matching the present composition of Belmont Park's dirt track, its time on the former surface was two seconds longer.

With enough such data, if the presumed slowing actually occurred, it should be possible to gain a fairly accurate estimate of how much slower the older surface was, when compared with the current surface, relative to horses as opposed to robots.

The data could then be substantiated simply by comparing a significant number of running times of actual races, past and present.

Again, I do not know whether this method is feasible. However, something like it should at least be attempted in order to make an objective comparison of 'era effects' possible and thus, hopefully, end some of the spiteful diatribes over this issue which prove nothing.

Other than a relatively small and calculable effect that steel racing plates may have had over aluminum plates, one cannot reasonably expect any further major differences to exist between the possibly mythological and most certainly ill-defined but ubiquitous eras.

For we know in part, and we prophesy in part. But when that which
is perfect is come, then that which is in part will be done away . . .
For now we see through a glass, darkly; but then face to face; now
I know in part; but then shall I know even as also I am known.
-- 1 Corinthians 13: 9-10; 12

CHAPTER 10

Concluding Thoughts on Greatness

In chapter 9 the probability of a given horse demonstrating what I chose to define as its true greatness in twelve consecutive races was stated. The result equated to flipping an unbiased coin thirty-five consecutive times and getting either all tails or all heads. Numerically, the chance of that occurring was given as one in about 27.29 billion.

The reader will, I hope, forgive me if I now exit the juvenile year and enter the sophomore year momentarily to demonstrate an interesting fact. I believe it is worthy of consideration for those interested in further explorations of thoroughbred data analysis.

And it happens that the sophomore year of one particular horse, Secretariat, demonstrates this fact as elegantly as any of which I know.

To enhance this example, Figure 7 is now presented.

Figure 7
Kentucky Derby Trend Study: Two Eras

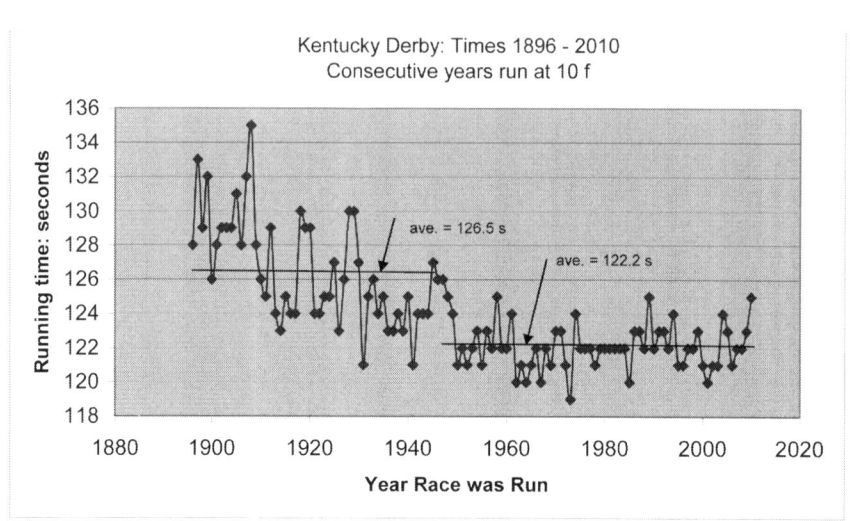

The run times for the Kentucky Derby, rounded to the nearest whole number for simplicity, are plotted in Figure 7 for the 115 consecutive years from 1896 through 2010. During this time, the Derby has been run at ten furlongs. It actually began in 1875, but it was run at twelve furlongs until 1896. Refer to The American Racing Manual 2005 (8).

Visually inspecting this graph seems to lead to the conclusion that the overall declining trend of the data shifts abruptly downward about the mid 1940s. Perhaps it is a coincidence, but author Richard Sowers (10), quoted previously, defines the beginning of the 'modern era' in thoroughbred racing as 1946.

I suggest you read at least the preface to his book to learn his reasons for selecting that date, since I feel that a discussion of them herein would be too distracting from the principal topic. It is nonetheless interesting that the level of the graph in Figure 7 does essentially seem to drop about that year.

Based on this brief introduction, I decided to call the years 1896 through 1945 'era one,' and the years from 1946 through 2010 'era two.'

Thus, the horizontal line indicated as 'ave. = 126.5 s' in Figure 7 represents the average of the integer run times for the first fifty years of the Kentucky Derby. Similarly, the lower horizontal line indicated as 'ave. = 122.2 s' in Figure 7 shows the average of the integer run times for the years 1946 through 2010. There are sixty-five such points.

Direct subtraction of these two averages indicates that the average running time for the Kentucky Derby dropped by 4.3 seconds between the two assumed eras.

It seems most logical to posit that both a change in track surface conditions and selective breeding are mainly responsible for this 4.3-second decrease in average running times. The only other remotely viable factor might be the weight difference between steel racing plates and aluminum plates, as previously mentioned.

Estimating a one-pound difference between the sets of steel and aluminum plates, one finds that, for a ten-furlong race, a maximum of 0.48 s can theoretically be lost by a horse wearing steel versus aluminum plates, if all else remains constant.

This calculation assumes that the weigh-in weight was 126 pounds, plate weight naturally not included, for the winning horse and that he ran the ten furlongs in 122.00 s – near the average running time for the 'modern era' shown in Figure 7.

With aluminum plates, the horse will actually carry about 126.8 pounds. With steel plates, the actual carried weight will be about 127.8 pounds. If one applies the kinetic energy formula using these two weights, one obtains the 0.48 s difference in run time due to the effect of the heavier steel plates.

This estimate is based on realistic weights. Beginning in 1920, the year in which Paul Jones won the Derby, since Man o' War did not enter that year, every winning colt has carried 126 pounds. The two winning fillies, in 1980 and 1988, carried 121 pounds.

However, for simplicity, assume that plate weights do not affect performance at all. When the standard deviations for the two eras are calculated, the results are 3.151 s for the earlier era and 1.474 s for the later era.

Taking the minus three-sigma level from these figures – that is, the average for each era minus three times its individual standard deviation

– one finds it is 117.05 s for the earlier era and 117.80 s (both values rounded to two decimal places) for the later era.

Now calculate the actual 'trip' made by Secretariat in winning the 1973 Derby, and you will find that he ran *at least* 105 feet further than the nominal Derby distance of 6,600 ft, or ten furlongs.

The 105 ft is accounted for by both his extra distance in coming from gate number ten to near the rail and then running at least fifteen feet from the rail around both the clubhouse and backstretch turns. Each turn at Churchill Downs is about 0.266 miles around. That distance translates to 1404.50 ft. For each foot increase in radius around a semi-circular turn (i.e., how much farther from the rail a horse runs around the turn) the horse adds an extra 3.14 ft, the value of pi, to the distance he or she runs.

Thus, Secretariat, estimated to have been *at least* fifteen feet from the rail, added at least 3.14 multiplied by 15, or 47.10 ft to the distance he ran around *each* of the two turns –clubhouse and backstretch.

Thus, instead of running the nominal ten-furlong distance in 119.40 s, as he is officially credited, he actually ran at least 6705 ft in 119.40 s. That makes his actual average speed 56.156 ft/s. That, in turn, makes the time he would have run 6600 ft, had he held the rail throughout, only 117.53 s.

He ran that race, therefore, very near the theoretical minus three-sigma limit (for either era) discussed in the last chapter. Compared to horses from the earlier era, his z-score (basically identical to cumulative standard deviations) was -2.85. Compared to the horses of the later era, his z-score was -3.17. He therefore ran *faster* compared to the so-called modern horses than he did compared to the earlier era horses. This fact is interesting, and bears comment a bit later.

For now, let us examine Secretariat's performance in the Preakness and the Belmont. Separate graphs of the trends for those two races will not be given because they show much similarity to the Kentucky Derby trend of Figure 7.

Suffice it to say that the Preakness has been run at nine and a-half furlongs since 1925. The Belmont has been run at twelve furlongs since 1926. Therefore, ample data exist for those races to make the same essential comparisons between two eras as was done for the Derby – despite the fact that the Derby stayed at a constant distance for a much longer time.

Regarding the Preakness, it must first be noted that the Maryland Racing Commission fairly recently decided not to review Secretariat's Preakness time and credits him with the time of 114.4 s. (19) However, enough independent evidence exists, in my opinion, to indicate that he should be credited with the faster time of 113.4 s accepted by and officially listed in the Daily Racing Form. (3)

The reader may reach his or her own conclusions regarding this point.

When the Preakness trend beginning in 1925 and ending in 2010 is divided into the two eras as was the Derby, one finds that the average running time for the earlier era (1925 through 1945) is 119.33 s while the standard deviation for that era is 1.354 s. This makes the minus three-sigma value for the earlier era 115.27 s.

The average running time for the later era (1946 through 2010) is 115.74 s, and the standard deviation is 1.726 s. This makes the minus three-sigma level for that era 110.56 s.

Now, performing the same type calculations for Secretariat's Preakness 'trip' as were done for the Kentucky Derby, one finds that he actually would have run the nominal distance of 6270 ft (i.e., nine and a-half furlongs) at an average speed of 56.17 ft/s since he again ran at least fifteen feet wide of the rail on both turns.

This adjusted speed gives the time of 111.62 s in which he would actually have run the nominal distance. That time makes his z-score an incredible -5.69 for the older era and -2.39 for the later era. For the Preakness, Secretariat ran faster relative to the *older era* horses – a reversal of his Kentucky Derby performance. This result highlights inconsistencies for any era type arguments. The Derby case indicates that earlier era horses performed *better relative to Secretariat* than did modern ones. Thus, it seems at least questionable that those horses were hampered as much as cited by poor track conditions. Let the *Onus Probandi* rest as it may.

Regarding these speed adjustments, it is not unreasonable to assume a distance even farther from the rail than the estimated fifteen feet. That naturally puts Secretariat nearer the minus three-sigma level for the more modern era. One would, however, need to perform some special measurement estimates from old film footage to determine the exact distance. That may be impractical or impossible.

Suffice it to say that Secretariat was close to the lowest practical thoroughbred time limit for the first two 'jewels' of the Triple Crown – based on probability estimates of normal distributions for all the thoroughbreds having competed in these two races at their present running distance.

The story for the Belmont is easier to calculate than for the Derby or the Preakness because Secretariat held the rail for the entire trip. Therefore, he did run as close to the nominal race distance, 7920 ft for twelve furlongs, as was feasible.

His time for that win, by 31 lengths, was a flat 144.00 s. It is still the stakes record, the track record and the world record on dirt at that distance. It has now held for thirty-eight years – since the 2010 Belmont was just run in the plodding time of 2:31.57 by Drosselmeyer. This is nearly *eight seconds slower* than Secretariat's record time, but virtually nobody questions an era effect between Secretariat and Drosselmeyer!

The average for the 85 values of run times for the Belmont from 1926 through 2010 is 149.22 s. The standard deviation for those same times is 1.841 s. The minus three-sigma level is 143.70 s.

Secretariat's z-score based on his 144.00 s run time is -2.84. This is the same as saying that his standard deviation compared with *every thoroughbred* that ran the Belmont since 1926 is near its lowest practical theoretical limit – i.e., based on proportions to be expected under the normal curve.

If the earlier suggested definition of inherent greatness being manifest by performances at or near the minus three-sigma level is remotely valid, then Secretariat, for the Triple Crown at least, was, arguably and mathematically, near perfection.

The Fairness of Era Comparisons

Given the preceding facts about the Triple Crown races and how two distinct levels of average running times seem to naturally appear in their graphs, is it remotely fair to think that a so-called 'standard horse,' representative of the earlier era, could compete with a standard horse of the later era? There is an easy way to check this.

We simply perform a random number generation of one hundred hypothetical match races for both levels of each of the Triple Crown races using the averages and standard deviations appropriate to each of the artificial eras defined on the graphs.

Although the actual graphs for the Preakness and the Belmont were not presented, their averages and standard deviations, as used in Excel's Random Number Generator application, are given below.

If the hypothetical horse from the earlier era wins *any races* when thus matched against the hypothetical horse from the later era, then it cannot categorically be stated that one cannot compare horses from different eras. It is that simple. We revert again to the time-honored scientific principle of one refuting instance of a presumed 'truth' negating the status of a potential theory or law.

One may still claim that comparisons cannot be made between eras. However, that claim reverberates quite hollow, for comparisons can be made with proper adjustments. The following facts will indicate that this is sound reasoning.

Of course other mitigating factors must enter. However, it will be instructive to see what results are obtained simply by this very basic assumption regarding unadjusted era comparisons when combined with the technique of random number generation.

Old-Era Horse Versus New-Era Horse

With that intent, the averages and standard deviations of the two eras for each of the Triple Crown races, and the years for which the data are included, are listed below.

	Kentucky Derby	Preakness	Belmont
Years:	1896 -1945	1925 -1945	1926 - 1945
Average:	126.50 s	119.33 s	150.80 s
Std. Dev.:	3.151 s	1.354 s	1.609 s
Years:	1946 -2010	1946 – 2010	1946 - 2010
Average:	122.22 s	115.74 s	148.74 s
Std. Dev.:	1.474 s	1.726 s	1.632 s

When three consecutive simulations were performed for each race, the results were as given below. The numbers show how many wins the hypothetical standard horse representing each era would garner and, hence by implication, how many losses it would suffer, based on one hundred randomly generated match races per simulation.

	Kentucky Derby	Preakness	Belmont
Older Era:	12, 13, 15	3, 5, 8	15, 12, 10
Later Era:	88, 87, 85	97, 95, 92	85, 88, 90

While the wins for the older era's hypothetical standard horse are, as expected, fewer, this confirms that it is *not a priori correct* to say that one cannot directly compare horses from two eras or generations. The 'older' horses occasionally win!

If the non-comparison argument were strictly true, it would imply that the horse from the older generation would never have a chance of winning in comparison with a more modern horse. The data do not support such a conclusion, although the number of wins is admittedly small.

Another Era Simulation with Two Adjustments

Let us make two adjustments to all the running times from the older era data of the Kentucky Derby. A subtraction of 0.50 s for the plate weight of steel is performed, and another fifty-three percent of the remainder of the time difference between eras is subtracted, as Figure 7 indicates is needed, to approximate the foal crop effect.

In GHA, foal crop size was estimated to contribute from about seventy to eighty percent of the changes (lowering) of average decade running times in four major races. Fifty-three percent is used in this example because it allows subtracting an even number of seconds from the Kentucky Derby times, and it does not assume the full possible effect of foal crop. It is, thus, a conservative estimate.

Any residual effect could possibly originate from the track surface, but we cannot know that figure because valid measurements are lacking. More discussion follows on this topic near this chapter's conclusion.

Recall that a 4.3 s discrepancy exists between the average running times of the Kentucky Derby between the era of 1896 through 1945 and the era of 1946 through 2010.

The two adjustments to the earlier times thus introduced result in 2.50 s being subtracted from each older-era Derby running time. This procedure reduces the average running time of the earlier era from 126.50 s to 124.00 s. The standard deviation of the era remains un-changed. The reader is encouraged to verify that mathematical fact.

When a random simulation of one hundred races between the hy-pothetical standard horse from the *adjusted older era* with the stan-dard horse of the modern era is run, the result is that the older-era horse is now predicted to win thirty-six of one hundred races. This is a radical change.

It indicates that, if a full seventy-five to eighty percent adjustment for foal crop size effect were made, it is likely that the older era horse would be close to breaking even with the modern horse in predicted races won. The reader might check this also.

This entire discussion implies that *by no means* must one assume that the Kentucky Derby track surface of the older era *was totally re-sponsible*, or necessarily bore the greater responsibility, for slower run-ning times. Furthermore, one sees that it is fairly easy to make unbiased comparisons, through proper and non-biased data adjustment, of older eras with modern eras in the sport of thoroughbred racing.

The above discussion obviously will not convince those who wish not to be convinced that one cannot compare horses from different eras.

However, only a finite number of factors could possibly have been operative to define those eras. This example has basically accounted for a substantial fraction of the running time difference merely by adjusting two of the factors – the effect due to different racing plates and the foal crop effect wherein genetic improvements in the breed over time purportedly generate faster runners having more stamina.

We end this discussion and the book with a last look at the problem of measuring track surface effects.

The Problem: Defining a Standard Track Surface

In any accepted field of science, a standard is defined against which measurements of entities unrelated to the standard, but of similar nature, are made.

In the area of temperature measurement, for example, a standard thermometer can be constructed and a standard zero reference point of temperature on that thermometer can be established and marked.

That standard is called absolute zero on the Kelvin scale used by scientists in fields like thermodynamics and physical chemistry, and it is equivalent to approximately -273 degrees Kelvin or Centigrade (technically, -273.16° Kelvin). Absolute zero is defined as *the temperature at which all molecular motion ceases.*

This implies that if the temperature of some substance being tested (measured) is above -273 Celsius, then the molecular motion of that substance is greater, as it must be by definition, than the total absence of molecular motion implied by absolute zero.

In fact, the *kinetic energy* of molecules *is* the very property which makes the temperature of various substances in various phases – solid, liquid or gas – higher than absolute zero. That energy is expressed exactly by the same formula used for plate weight adjustments except that in thermometry the masses have the tiny values of molecules.

In essence, the *average kinetic energy of a group of molecules or atoms* **is** *the temperature of the substance comprised of those molecules or atoms.*

This extended discussion was necessary to prepare for thinking scientifically about track surfaces and their relation to or their affect on a horse's speed.

Almost immediately the astute reader will have asked about where a standard horse can be found (analogous to the standard thermometer) that can run on a standard surface (analogous to the condition of absolute zero) to establish a baseline equivalent to that used in thermometry.

The quick answer is that ***no such horse or surface exists***.

Think about that statement. If you understand it, it will open up a different view for you concerning the era and comparison debate, or similar debates.

How could one determine, or where could one find, for instance, a horse of which one could be assured that he was running at his absolute top speed on a given surface in order that his speed on other surfaces could later be directly compared with it?

It is impossible. For one thing, no real horse can maintain his or her absolute maximum speed for long, even if one knew the horse had reached it. He can't tell you!

Or, reversing the problem, how could one know when a surface was prepared so that it would enable any horse to run at his top speed for any really effective distance? What would its composition and density be? Again, the horse can't tell you.

The problem thus presents, at minimum, a two-edged sword of impossibility.

The only thing one can do, as was suggested in chapter 9, is to establish relative standards of track surface speed and somehow relate those to how they affect the general running speed of various horses.

It is, therefore, in principle, impossible to state that racetracks were generally four or five or any number of seconds slower in decades past than they are now. There is no absolute zero of track speed – or resistance – against which to measure and compare them. There exists no standard horse to run on them even if they did exist.

Yet such numbers relating to track speeds are bandied about willy-nilly by so-called racing gurus. They are by no means absolute and are essentially meaningless.

Would any horse you care to name have *necessarily run*, say, four seconds slower on the Belmont Park track of 1925 than he would on the present Belmont Park track today under the same impost and length of run? Nobody knows that, and no data exist to support or negate the statement. It doesn't matter what the average and standard deviation of the Belmont Park track was in 1925. Each horse reacted differently to it. That difference essentially is shown by the standard deviation over numerous races.

The problem is indeed aggravating, but it is important to separate what can from what cannot justly be said about comparing running horses.

This is as good a point as any to conclude a book about equine greatness. Hopefully several things have been stated herein that will motivate some readers to study thoroughbred racing in greater detail and try to make genuine contributions to the clarification of data analysis peculiar to that realm. The industry sorely needs it.

As stated previously, we do not measure the inherent ability of a Thoroughbred by performing statistical analyses on the data he or she leaves for posterity. No such claim is being offered that anything presented herein remotely does that.

Past performance data – merely dark symbols on the lighter background of moldering racing chronicles – are like the sooty residue of a magnificent fire which was once the creature's soul.

The fire's nature was and is forever beyond our ken. Its residue of shadowy ciphers, all that we frail humans are allowed to view, is merely an intimation – distorted by the lens of human measurement within the artificial systems of amusement humans devise to yield those measurements – of their magnificent source.

Greatness is now a highly overworked and largely meaningless expression, often applied casually and flippantly.

Once upon a time, when society overall was more ingenuous, the term meant that something or somebody was truly an outstanding exemplar of their class – an epitome, if you will.

It is now more akin to expressions such as 'awesome,' which can signify nearly any level of quality or lack thereof, depending upon the observer and the proclaimer.

Not many years ago I took a written drivers examination. I missed one question and was miffed by my sloppiness. However, my score so impressed the lady who graded the examination – perhaps a sorry comment on societal standards in itself – that she called her younger colleague over to tell her of my singular misstep.

"Awesome!" the young woman declared.

I cringed inwardly, accepted my license renewal and walked away.

ACKNOWLEDGMENTS

Grateful acknowledgment is hereby given to Ms. Heather Rohde who designed the cover and created the superb portraits of Colin, Man o' War, Ruffian and Landaluce which grace their respective chapters' initial pages.

Ms. Rohde may be reached via her web site: www.rohdefineart.com

I also acknowledge and thank Mr. Allan Carter, Historian of the National Museum of Racing and Hall of Fame for supplying important vital statistics for the filly First Flight.

Last, but not least, my thanks to Bob DeGroff and Team Gambia at Author House for designing a professional text.

Notes

1 All Biblical quotations herein are from the King James Bible printed by Thomas Nelson & Sons, Fourth Avenue Building, 381-385 Fourth Avenue, New Your, New York.

2 All comment lines cited herein are from the Daily Racing Form's 2000 publication, Champions, unless otherwise noted.

3 "Colin." *Wikipedia: The Free Encyclopedia.* Wikimedia Foundation, Inc. 14 Jan. 2010. Web. 13 Mar. 2010. <http://en.wikipedia.org/wiki/Colin_(horse)>

Figures and Tables

Bibliography

1.   Justice, Charles. <u>The Greatest Horse of All: A Controversy Examined.</u> Bloomington, Indiana: Author House, 2008.

2.   The Blood-Horse. <u>Thoroughbred Champions: Top 100 Racehorses of the 20th Century.</u> Lexington, Kentucky: The Blood-Horse, Inc., 1999.

3.   Daily Racing Form LLC. <u>Champions.</u> New York: Daily Racing Form Press, 2000.

4.   Walpole, Ronald E., and Myers, Raymond H., <u>Probability and Statistics for Engineers and Scientists, 3rd. ed.,</u> New York: Macmillan Publishing Company, 1985.

5.   Hollingsworth, Kent (Editor). <u>The Great Ones.</u> Lexington, Kentucky: The Blood-Horse, 1970.

6.   Sgt. Ted Smout, Australian Medical Corps., quoted in <u>Wikipedia, http://en.wikipedia.org/wiki/Manfred_von_Richthofen</u>, 2010.

7.   Ours, Dorothy. <u>Man o' War, A Legend Like Lightning</u>. New York: St. Martin's Press, 2006.

8.   Daily Racing Form LLC. <u>The American Racing Manual 2005.</u> New York: Daily Racing Form Press, 2005.

9.   Schmuller, Joseph. <u>Statistical Analysis with Excel for Dummies.</u> Hoboken, New Jersey: Wiley Publishing, Inc., 2005

10.   Sowers, Richard. <u>The Abstract Primer of Thoroughbred Racing</u>. Stockbridge, Georgia: Old Sport Publishing Company, 2004.

11. Schwartz, Jane. <u>Ruffian: Burning from the Start</u>. 1991. New York: Random House, Inc., 2002.

12. Toby, Milton C. <u>Ruffian.</u> Thoroughbred Legends, number 13. Lexington, Kentucky: Eclipse Press, 2003.

13. Legrand, Michel. <u>Brian's Song.</u> COLGEMS-EMI MUSIC INC. 1972

14. Isenberg, Jerry. Star-Ledger, Newark, NJ. <u>Secretariat's Belmont: Part 2.</u> ESPN Classic, 2000.

15. Carter, Allan. "Re: First Flight." E-mail to Charles Justice. 10 May 2010.

16. Bloom, Allen David (translator). <u>The Republic of Plato.</u> 2nd ed., 7.514a – 7.521a) New York: Basic Books, 1991

17. Jockey Club Fact Book. "Annual North American Registered Foal Crop by Decade." Online posting. 18 March 2010. <u>http://www.equineonline.com/factbook/foalcrop-nabd.html</u>.

18. Hollingsworth, Kent. <u>The Kentucky Thoroughbred.</u> Lexington, Kentucky: The University Press of Kentucky, 1985.

19. Hopkins, J. Michael. "Re: Secretariat's Official Preakness Time." E-mail to Charles Justice. 19 June 2007.

Appendix A: Calculating the Standard Deviation

Microsoft Excel calculates standard deviations for you – provided you ask it nicely! However, it is wise to learn the manual procedure. Therefore, the following set of thirteen data points is given, and the method of calculating the standard deviation from them is explained.

The data are the running times for the filly Imp. She was foaled in 1894 and had the remarkable lifetime record of 171 starts with 62 wins, 35 places and 29 shows. She was thus 'on the board' for seventy-four percent of her races.

These data represent only the times for her six-furlong races on fast rated tracks for the year 1897. She had thirteen such races, hence the sample size n = 13. She won the four highlighted races.

Date	Time (seconds)	Deviation	Dev^2	R	SD
28 Apr	**74.50**	0.37	0.1352	8.2680	±0.830
18 May	74.54	0.41	0.1662	= Σ Dev^2/12	
29 May	73.82	-0.31	0.0975	= 0.689	
1 Jun	**74.00**	-0.13	0.0175		
10 Jun	74.63	0.50	0.2477	SD = $\sqrt{0.689}$	
1 Jul	74.88	0.75	0.5590	= ±0.830	
11 Aug	74.20	0.07	0.0046		
28 Aug	72.82	-1.31	1.7222		
2 Sep	**73.00**	-1.13	1.2821		

11 Sep	**73.25**	-0.88	0.7785
15 Sep	75.49	1.36	1.8433
16 Oct	73.47	-0.66	0.4387
21 Oct	75.12	0.99	0.9755

The standard deviation calculation of Imp's thirteen run times begins by finding their average. Therefore, add the thirteen run times and divide their sum by thirteen. The result, to two decimal places, is 74.13.

Now calculate what is called the deviation score for each of the thirteen separate run times. To do this, subtract the average just calculated from each run time. List the results, as in the third column labeled 'Deviation,' above. Negative values are normal. Don't worry about them.

Square each deviation score and list the results, as in the column labeled 'Dev^2' All these values have been rounded to four decimal places. Squaring makes them all positive, and this is desired. See, I told you not to worry about those negative signs!

Now, add all the Dev^2 scores. Divide that total by (n – 1), that is the sample size minus 1, which is 12. The answer is listed in the fifth column above, labeled 'R' for result.

You're nearly done. Take the square root of R. The answer is in the column labeled 'SD.'

And that's all there is to calculating the standard deviation, ±0.830 in this example. Recall that square roots always imply both a negative and a positive answer, hence the ±.

Now think about what you just calculated. The standard deviation is one of the most critical numbers in all of statistics. It applies to a normal distribution of scores or measurements, no matter what you are measuring. It also applies to other distributions.

In Imp's case, the measurements were her run times for six furlongs, all on fast tracks.

These thirteen run times were tested for normalcy using the Shapiro-Wilk test. It is beyond the scope of this book to explain that test. Let it suffice to state that the test indicated the thirteen run times had a probability of 0.9917 (1.00 being 100 percent) of being from a normal distribution. So we assume they are normally distributed.

That's excellent because it allows us to state the following:

Based on her standard deviation just calculated, Imp would probably never have run a six-furlong race on a fast track in *more than* 76.62 seconds – at least under her typical imposts. This value is just her average *plus* three times her standard deviation. That is, it is 74.13 + 3(0.830) = 76.62.

Likewise, she probably never would have run a six-furlong race on a fast track in *less than* 71.64 seconds. That value is, as you might surmise, her average *minus* three times her standard deviation. That is, it is 74.13 – 3(0.830) = 71.64.

The odds of her being beyond those two limits, called the 'three-sigma limits,' would be a very slim 0.27 percent. That's close enough for government work, as some wags would suggest. These odds are based on the mathematical nature of the normal curve itself.

Knowing that her run time distribution for six furlongs is normal, plus both her average and standard deviation, thus gives a powerful insight into her capabilities for running this distance.

Based on this knowledge, computer-simulated match races between her and any other horse, colt or filly, for which equivalent information exists, can be generated.

These simulations, as used herein, yield a very good estimate of how many match races of 100, using a convenient number, one horse would likely win over another.

That information, in turn, facilitates in settling disputes over which horse was 'greater' than another. It is an objective, scientific evaluation as opposed to pure speculation.

Appendix B: Input and Output for the Futurity Single-Factor ANOVA

Given four track conditions

<u>INPUTS</u>

Sheepshead Bay	Saratoga	Belmont Pre-improved	Belmont Post-improved
74.00	72.20	71.80	71.60
73.00	75.00	73.80	72.20
71.80	76.80	72.00	71.40
71.80		72.80	71.00
73.60			70.40
71.20			70.80
71.20			
71.80			
Mean 72.30	74.67	72.60	71.23
N 8	3	4	6

<u>OUTPUTS</u>

SUMMARY

Groups	Count	Sum	Average	Variance
Sheepshead Bay	8	578.4	72.30	1.1771

159

Saratoga	3	224	74.67	5.3733
Pre-improved Belmont	4	290.4	72.60	0.8267
Post-improved Belmont	6	427.4	71.23	0.4067

ANOVA

Source of Variation	SS	df	MS	F	P-value	F critical
Between Groups	23.81	3	7.939	5.74	0.00667	3.19678
Within Groups	23.5	17	1.382			
Total	47.32	20				

Note: The P-value indicates that the null hypothesis that all four means are equal may be rejected with less than seven chances in one thousand of being in error.

Appendix C: Abbreviated Table of t Values

Significance level for the one-tailed t test

.10	.05	.025	.01	.005	.0005

Significance level for the two-tailed t test

df	.20	.10	.05	.02	.01	.001
1	3.078	6.314	12.706	31.821	63.657	636.619
2	1.886	2.920	4.303	6.965	9.925	31.598
3	1.638	2.353	3.182	4.541	5.841	12.941
4	1.533	2.132	2.776	3.747	4.604	8.610
5	1.476	2.015	2.571	3.365	4.032	6.859
6	1.440	1.943	2.447	3.143	3.707	5.959
7	1.415	1.895	2.635	2.998	3.499	5.405
8	1.397	1.860	2.306	2.896	3.355	5.041
9	1.383	1.833	2.262	2.821	3.250	4.781
10	1.372	1.812	2.228	2.764	3.169	4.587
11	1.363	1.796	2.201	2.718	3.106	4.437
12	1.356	1.782	2.179	2.681	3.055	4.318
13	1.350	1.771	2.160	2.650	3.012	4.221
14	1.345	1.761	2.145	2.624	2.977	4.140
15	1.341	1.753	2.131	2.602	2.947	4.073

16	1.337	1.746	2.120	2.583	2.921	4.015
17	1.333	1.740	2.110	2.567	2.898	3.965
18	1.330	1.734	2.101	2.552	2.878	3.922
19	1.328	1.729	2.093	2.539	2.861	3.883
20	1.325	1.725	2.086	2.528	2.845	3.850
25	1.316	1.708	2.060	2.485	2.787	3.725
30	1.310	1.697	2.042	2.457	2.750	3.646
40	1.303	1.684	2.021	2.423	2.704	3.551
60	1.296	1.671	2.000	2.390	2.660	3.460

Note: The term 'df' means degrees of freedom. To find the df value for two samples, add the number of data items in each sample and then subtract 2. In equation form this is df = n_1 + n_2 – 2. For example if sample one contains 10 items and sample two contains 7 items, then df = 10 + 7 – 2 = 15.

INDEX

linear trend, 51; and t test, 56; and modified running times, 60; and linear estimate comparison, 61; and predicted times for six furlongs, 62

Colitis X, 86, 87

Combinations, and formula, 10

Commando, 18

Comparison factors Colin and Man o' War, 47; and career records, 48; and fastest average speed in a race, 48; and greatest momentum in a race, 48; and greatest action in a race, 48; and imposts, 49; and average momentum, 49; and average action, 49; and average winning margins, 49; and average field size, 49; and average post position, 49; and average performance figure, 50; and average track record comparison, 50; and Ruffian and Landaluce, 91; and general, 92

Copernica, 75

1 Corinthians, quotation, 133

Correlation, general, 10; negative and meaning, 12; positive and meaning, 12

D

Daily Racing Form, Champions, 4, 41, 72, 77; and Secretariat, 137

Damascus, 2, 4, 7; and z-score, 8; and general, 27; and ancestor of Personal Ensign, 118

Darebin, 18; and Lawrence Realization, 18

Dark Star, 72

Degrees of freedom (df), 58

Del Mar, track, 84; and Debutante Stakes, 84

DeMoivre, Abraham, and normal distribution equation, 13

Dependent variable, 4, 12

Direct relationship, and meaning, 12

Discovery, 72

Dominique, 32

Domino, 17

Dr. Fager, 2, 4, 7; and z-score, 8

Drosselmeyer, and 2010 Belmont Stakes, 138

E

Ecclesiastes, quotation, 119

Eclipse Stakes, 19, 20

Einstein, Albert, 123

H

Hail to Reason, 82

Harbut, Will, 30, 42

Hasten On, 39

Hedevar, 7

Himyar, 17

Hira Villa Stud, 17, 18

Hoist the Flag, ancestor of Personal Ensign, 118

Hollingsworth, Kent, 27; and percent of stakes winners from foal crop, 129

Hollywood Lassie Stakes, 83

Hollywood Park, and Landaluce, 82, 83, 88

Hollywood Starlet Stakes, 87

Honorable mention, Thoroughbreds, 105, 112

Hoodwink, 32

Hopeful Stakes, 40

Hot n Nasty, 77

Hudson Stakes, 34

I

Impost, 9, 25

Independent variable, 4, 12

Intelligence, as a human trait, 120

Inverse relationship, and meaning, 12

Izenberg, Jerry, and Newark Star-Ledger, 89

J

Jamaica, track, 33, 34

Janney, Barbara, 73

Janney, Stuart S., 73

Jeffords, Sarah, 38

Jim Gaffney, 22

Jockey Club Fact Book, and foal crops, 129

John P. Greer, 41, 56

K

Keene, Foxhall, 108

Keene, James R., 18, 108

Keene Memorial Stakes, 32

Kelso, 72

Kentucky Derby, xix, 42; and Native Dancer, 72; and Secretariat's z-score, 128; and general trend, 134, 135; and era comparisons chart, 140

Kinetic energy, 34, 48; and calculation of, 63; and relation to momentum, 93; and formula for, 99, 135

Korzybski, Alfred, xxi

Kummer, Clarence, 39

L

Landaluce, and Ruffian, 69; and biography, 81; and name origin, 81; and pedigree, 82; and maiden race, 82; and average winning margins, 82; and Hollywood Lassie Stakes, 83; and Del Mar Debutante Stakes, 84; and Santa Anita Anoakia Stakes, 85; and Santa Anita Oak Leaf Stakes, 87; and death, 88; burial, 88; and Champion 2yo Filly, 82, 88

Landaluce, Francisco, 81

La Prevoyante, 69, 107, 112; and Spinaway, 78; and career record, 115; and linear trend predictions, 115; and Dr. Fager's record mile, 116; and Miss Florida Handicap, 116; and death, 116; and honors, 116

Laughing Bridge, 76, 78

Lauren, Lucien, and quotation about Ruffian, 79

Laws of physics, 123

Length, definition, 34

Lexington, Kentucky, 17; and Castleton Stud, 18; and August Belmont, 29; and Faraway Farms, 42, 43

Limits analysis, 13; and three-sigma analysis, 13; and area under normal curve, 13; and linear trends, 45; and Colin, 64; and Man o' War, 64; and NORMDIST function, 65, 66, 67; and random number generation, 67; and six-furlong races, 100, 105; and normal distribution, 101, 102; and Ruffian, 105

Linear regression, 3, 4, 15; and Buckpasser, 5

Linear Trend Analysis, and Man o' War, 42; and related methods, 45; and Colin versus Man o' War, 51; and the Belmont Stakes, 60; and t test adjustments, 64

Linear trend, general, xix; and example, 3

LINEST function, 111

LINEST routine, and Excel, 4, 5

Locust Hill Farm, 73

Loftus, John, 31; and barrier, 31, 32, 33, 35, 37, 38, 39; and last race with Man o' War, 41

Loftus, Margaret O'Dowd, 41

Lukas, D. Wayne, 82, 87, 88

M

Mahmoud, sire of First Flight, 112

Mahubah, dam of Man o' War, 29

Mannie Gray, 17

Man o' War, 29, 30; and momentum, 48; and biography, 29; and name origin, 30; and Will Harbut, 30, 42; and barrier, 32, 48; and nickname Red, 34; and imposts, 34; and weight gain, 35; and nickname Big Red, 34; and barrier controversy, 37; and loss to Upset, 38; and final juvenile race, 41; and Preakness, 42; as 3yo and Kentucky Derby, 43; and honors, 43; and death, 43; and linear trend, 45, 51; and Futurity, 53; and John P. Greer, 56; and linear estimate comparison, 60; and six-furlong races, 62; and normal distribution, 65; and predicted times for standard distances, 111; and race continuity, 125; and Travers, 127; and z-score comparison with Secretariat, 125, 126

Margin, winning, average for all races, Colin and Man o' War, 49

Matron Stakes, 18, 24, 25

McKinley, William, president and assassination of, 17

Meelick, 21

Melton Mowbray, town, 108

Middleburg, Virginia, 27, 29

Miller, Walter, 19, 20, 22

Momentum, calculation of, 26; and highest, 48; and average for all races, 49

Monmouth Park, 77

Most races, same distance, Colin and Man o' War, 49

My Laddie, 32

Myrtle Charm, 82

N

Nasrullah, 82

National Museum of Racing Hall of Fame, 27, 116, 118

National Stallion Stakes, 19

R

S

Variable, independent, 4, 12

Variant, track, 9, 12, 20, 50; and Ruffian, 76; and Sorority Stakes, 77

Vasquez, Jacinto, 73, 74, 75, 77, 78

Vietnam War, 71

Violet Tip, 35

Von Richthofen, Lothar, 29

Von Richthofen, Manfred, 29, 31

W

War Admiral, and relation to Personal Ensign, 118

Watergate, and break-in, 71

Weight (impost), and average carried, 9; and correlations, 38; and momentum, 48; and Kinetic energy, 63

Wheeler, Bob, 73

Whiteley, Frank Y., 73, 74; and not setting Ruffian down, 75

Widener Course, and Belmont Park, 113

Woodward stakes, 1967, 2

Y

y-intercept, and linear trend, 4

Youthful Stakes, 33

Z

z-score, 8; and Thoroughbred greatness, 125; and Travers and Man o' War, 127; and explanation of, 125; and calculating, 126; and comparing Man o' War to Secretariat, 127; and t test, 128

ABOUT THE AUTHOR

Charles Justice is a native Hoosier (despite that term's ambiguity), born in Vincennes, Indiana and raised in Terre Haute, Indiana.

He holds an M.S. degree in physics and a Ph.D. in educational psychology. His study specialties within the latter field were applied statistical methods and the mental development of gifted children.

He has twenty years experience in general applied statistics with several major U.S. government facilities, including the Naval Research Laboratory in Washington, D.C.

He has held teaching positions in Electronics and Computer Technology at Indiana State University and in special education at McNeese State University.

In November 2008 he published his first Author House book, The Greatest Horse of All: A Controversy Examined.

He currently lives in Bloomington, Indiana with his wife Ann and three exemplary feline friends – Pepper, Sake and Cocoa.

His primary interests, alphabetically, include: clarinet, cosmology, model airplanes, photography, piano, pocket billiards, recreational mathematics, thoroughbred racing and writing.

Printed in Great Britain
by Amazon

37680618R00115